HIDDEN TREASURES

Co Down

Edited by Lucy Jeacock

First published in Great Britain in 2002 by
YOUNG WRITERS
Remus House,
Coltsfoot Drive,
Peterborough, PE2 9JX
Telephone (01733) 890066

HB ISBN 0 75433 814 2
SB ISBN 0 75433 815 0

FOREWORD

This year, the Young Writers' Hidden Treasures competition proudly presents a showcase of the best poetic talent from over 72,000 up-and-coming writers nationwide.

Young Writers was established in 1991 and we are still successful, even in today's technologically-led world, in promoting and encouraging the reading and writing of poetry.

The thought, effort, imagination and hard work put into each poem impressed us all, and once again, the task of selecting poems was a difficult one, but nevertheless, an enjoyable experience.

We hope you are as pleased as we are with the final selection and that you and your family continue to be entertained with *Hidden Treasures Co Down* for many years to come.

CONTENTS

Drumaness Primary School

Heather Bell	73
Matthew King	74
Gareth Wilson	74
Robert Bell	74
Holly Mitchell	75
Aaron Megaw	75
Jenny Waddell	75
Emma Jayne Johnston	76

Killyleagh Primary School

Ryan Wilkinson	76
Adam McClurg	77
Amber Marks	77
Stuart Cranston	78
Robert Ferguson	78
Timothy Morrison	79
Amy Collins	79
Tara Starbuck	80
Daryl Young	80
Johnathon Scott	81
Rachelle Ross	82
Steven Shields	82
Scott Rodgers	83
Christopher Graham	83
Phillip Ferguson	84

Milltown Primary School

Ryan Peden	84
Victoria Baird	85
Amelia White	85
Mark Peden	86
Matthew McAdam	86
Sarah Hazlett	87
Jenny Peden	88
Carrie Lennon	88
Sarah McAdam	89

Poyntzpass Primary School

Holly Lockhart	90
John Irvine	90
Hannah Liggett	91
Rebekah Denny	92
Mark Cairns	92
Kyle Walker	93
Louise Robinson	93
Amy Liggett	94
Alan Wilson	94
James Rooney	95
Stephanie Henry	95
Neil Anderson	96
Rachel Bryson	96
Cathy Wilson	96
Leanne Walker	97
Samantha Hazlett	98
Tyrone Linden	99
Sam Lockhart	100
Josh Ferris	101
Naomi Clarke	102
Sandra Meredith	103

Redburn Primary School

Andy Boal	104
Sarah-Jane Carruthers	104
Zoe McDevitt	105
Luke McCall	105
Gemma Kilby	106
Stewart Mitchell	106
Peter Murray	107
Hannah-Rose Henning	107
Sam Yates	108
Scott Rankin	108
Jonathan Jackson	109
Rachel Pardon	109

Tullymacarette Primary School

The Poems

THE TOY

Once there was a boy
Who had a special toy
That he played with every day.
'He's playing with that toy again,'
        his mum and dad would say.

For hours and hours he'd disappear
They'd call for him but he would not hear
Asked 'Have you your homework done?'
He'd reply 'No, I am having too much fun.'

To hide his toy would not be nice
But what would be your best advice?
He has to do his homework every night
Before he switches off his light!

Andrew Gibson (10)
Ballycloughan Primary School

PETS

Pets are cool
and some like it in the pool.
I like different animals
because they look cute.
They can be cats, dogs and birds.
They can be comfortable and reliable
just like me and you.

There's this cat that lives beside me.
His name is Buffy and he is so fluffy.
Buffy likes chewing his toys
and he likes playing with all of the boys.

Ana Howard (9)
Ballycloughan Primary School

SEASONS

Spring is when animals grow,
Winter is when there's ice and snow,
Summer is when the skies brighten up,
Autumn is when chestnuts drop.

Lambs are gallivanting around the field,
Many crops are going to yield.
The flowers open up one by one,
Opening for the bright, warm sun.

When the sun comes out to stay,
All the clouds drift away.
Birds chirp many, jolly, cheerful songs,
Sadly they don't sing all day long.

Pitter-patter, goes the rain,
Running down the windowpane,
All the leaves drifting down,
Floating silently to the ground.

Stiff and white, frigid freeze
Fresh and frosty, such a breeze!
Many birds fly a long journey south
To find something to fill their mouth.

Rebecca Gibson (11)
Ballycloughan Primary School

ELEPHANTS

If one hundred were found to board a bus,
Would the driver make a fuss?

If fifty elephants shopped in the spar,
Would the shopkeeper go bizarre?

If twenty elephants went to school together,
Would the teacher get in a tether?

And if one little elephant were to be my pet,
Would my mum let it stay
                        for just one day?

Kathryn Harrison (11)
Ballycloughan Primary School

BUBBLES

Dip the bubble stick
Into the frothy liquid,
And just like magic,
Round and colourful
Smooth and shiny
One appears, 1, 2, 3,
Oh such beauty sitting there,
Dangling off the end of the hoop,
Cheeky, refusing to go,
Then suddenly . . . pop!
It explodes in your face!

Dip the bubble stick again
Into the frothy liquid,
And blow gently,
Just like crystal,
Bubbles come all the time,
Each one glossy,
Smooth like hollow balls,
Shimmering as they go,
Gliding through the air,
Fragile, unreal,
Then disappear.

David McBriar (9)
Ballycloughan Primary School

FIRE!

There's a gleaming light,
Then there's red, orange, yellow, oh how bright!
It makes a warm, roomy glow,
The fire goes up and down in a flow.

You can warm your feet,
Against the hot, gleaming heat.
On the fire
Add some black peat.

Some toast would be good,
For warm, crunchy food.
When we've eaten it up,
We'll have tea, in a cup.

The flames have gone,
But not for long.
Tomorrow night,
They'll be back - golden and bright!

Michael Kinley (10)
Ballycloughan Primary School

MY GUITAR

My guitar arrived one frosty morning,
from yer man, Santa Claus!

My guitar, beautiful in design, Spanish,
from yer man, Santa Claus!

My guitar, I must learn to play quite hard,
My guitar I will learn to play,
Mrs Munro plays the guitar, some day I'll be better.

Catherine Rea (10)
Ballycloughan Primary School

THE WINTER POEM

Winter is coming, it is getting cold,
Ponds, streams and lakes will freeze, I am told.

Robins, blackbirds and all their little mates,
Get ready for the challenge that awaits.

Another stick here, and a feather there,
For their nests, a friend to make a pair.

Nuts from the garden, that were kindly left,
Berries from the bushes, they taste the best.

See the snowdrops, white and small,
Sitting behind our garden wall.

The nights are getting darker,
I can't see a thing,
But just around the corner,
Here comes *spring!*

Rachael Barr (10)
Ballycloughan Primary School

CARS, CARS

Cars, cars, ripping and roaring
Cars, cars, rallying and racing
Cars, cars, crashing and crumpling
Cars, cars, crunching and crippling
Cars, cars - are they so great?

Cars, cars, slow and slumping
Cars, cars, sad and broken
Towed away
No more bumping.

Richard Young (10)
Ballycloughan Primary School

FIREWORKS

Bright, dancing way up high
Shooting far into the sky
Never to be seen again
Hope this fun never ends.

Golds, silvers, reds and blues
These are all attractive
But dangerous too
Danger, danger, in the air
Watch out mums, mind your hair
Because these are dangerous
Don't be courageous
Be safe! Be sound!

David Carson (11)
Ballycloughan Primary School

A BONFIRE

We gathered fuel for the fire,
I struck a match and threw it on.
When it was lit, I had to admire,
So I gathered more fuel for the fire.

You could hear the fire crackling and sizzling outside the door,
And when I peered out of the window it needed fuel once more.
I ran outside and placed fuel to burn,
My dad came out and said, 'That's wrong, you'll have to learn.'

I watched the fire dwindle away,
And hoped for one another day.

Katie Spurr (10)
Ballycloughan Primary School

THE GHOST

Under inky black sky, littered with stars,
Lingers a ghost for hours and hours,
Rattles his chains, glows with spite,
As he drifts into the lonely night.

Heavy breathing, cackling laugh,
As he glides up your garden path,
By your bed, he'll hover and stand,
Looking glum but rather grand.

Who this is, you realise,
When you notice his beady eyes,
A mighty person - oh, so great,
Evil Henry number eight!

Shannah Kirke (11)
Ballycloughan Primary School

SNOW

Walking through the cold, crunchy white snow,
Where it all comes from, I don't know,
In the snow the children will play,
While the dogs in the barn rest in the hay.

The very next day,
We got out our sleigh,
On our sleigh we raced down a hill,
Up and down at our own free will.

We had such fun although it was cool,
But we were snug and warm in our clothes made of wool,
And then it got late and hunger came,
Can't wait till tomorrow to do it again.

Matthew Connolly (10)
Ballycloughan Primary School

FOUR SEASONS

Spring is here, spring is here,
Tulips, crocuses are now in bloom,
Calves, lambs are now all born,
Skipping and playing all day long.

Summer is here, summer is here.
Lovely golden sandy shore,
The clear, deep blue sea,
And children splashing all day long.

Autumn is here, autumn is here,
Reds, yellows, oranges and browns,
The trees are bare and cold,
And children kick the leaves.

Winter is here, winter is here,
Snow is falling, here and there,
As children build the snowmen,
And scurry around without a care.

Michael Morrow (10)
Ballycloughan Primary School

SUMMER

Summertime is here at last
We can put the winter in the past.
The grass is green and lush
Is that a rabbit I see in that bush?
The bees are buzzing all around

The birds look for worms underground.
The sun is shining, bright and warm
But beware of the rays so you come to no harm.
The flowers are growing bright and gay
Oh this is such a beautiful day.

Nathan Heaybourne (10)
Ballycloughan Primary School

ANIMALS ON THE FARM

Some animals sleep on hay,
Some just sleep in a den,
Some are working every day,
Some are in a pen.

From a farmyard cat,
To a small, smelly rat,
On the old rusty plough
To a milking free cow.

The wind howls with force,
Round a stable with a horse,
And a clucking pen,
With a snuggly hen.

The dotty dogs dig,
There's a smelly, clean pig,
The storm blows wisps of hay,
But all the animals had a wonderful day.

Rebecca Connolly (9)
Ballycloughan Primary School

WINTERTIME

Soft, white, falling snow,
Snow drifting to and fro,
Throwing a snowball up in the air,
To hit my snowman over there.

I run inside to get my tea,
There's lovely jelly made by me,
After that I go to bed,
Lying down, I rest my head.

Next day the snow has melted away,
It's hot and sunny here today,
I loved the snow while it was here,
Perhaps it will return again next year!

Bethan Leonard (10)
Ballycloughan Primary School

TIME MACHINE

Time machine, if only I had a time machine,
I could explore and see things no one has seen.
I could go to the future, I could go to the past,
I could go as far as my fuel would last.

I could go to the Vikings,
And start a big raid,
I could go to the Victorians,
To see what they made.

But where I'd like to go, best of all,
Is the future, where I'd have a ball!

Glenn Burton (11)
Ballyvester Primary School

HIDDEN TREASURE

H idden treasure is to be found
I n the desert underground.
D eep beneath the sandy floor
D ig and dig to find some more.
E very pirate tries to find
N ever-ending treasure underground.

T he treasure is under a big palm tree
R emember to find the rusty key.
E very tree needs to be searched
A part from the one where the parrot is perched.
S ure you'll find it, just search and search
U nder the sand beneath the birch.
R iches and glory it could bring
E very year I could be king.

Daniel Warwick (11)
Ballyvester Primary School

DISCOVERY

T is for *treasure* deep under the sea
R is for a *rusty* key found beside the chest
E is for *eels* that swim close by
A is for *after* on the old shipwreck
S is for *soon*, they have opened the chest
U is for *under* the gold they find the jewels
R is for *ring,* a pure gold ring
E is for *everyone,* I'll share it all with you.

Joshua David Johnson (11)
Ballyvester Primary School

CHRISTMAS

C hristmas is a frosty time
H ear the distant church bells chime
R oofs of houses packed with snow
I just hope it will never go
S hopping has all been done
T omorrow will be so much fun
M orning has come, Christmas is here
A ll the day to laugh and cheer
S oon it will be New Year's Day
      all the snow has gone away.

Conor Savage (11)
Ballyvester Primary School

JUST A DREAM

I was diving down to the ocean floor
And I found a hidden door,
The door was jammed and so was I
I thought that I was going to die
My air tank was fading away, away, away.

Then my alarm clock went off!
Another day!

Adam Connolly (10)
Ballyvester Primary School

HIDDEN TREASURE

Hidden treasure in the sea
Hidden treasure there for me
Round and round I look for the key
Hidden treasure just for me.

Finally I find the key
In a bunch of slimy weed
I open the chest and what do I see?
All the treasure I would need.

Cara Megson (11)
Ballyvester Primary School

HIDDEN TREASURE

The treasure is at the bottom of the sea,
And it is waiting just for me,
So I'll go on a scuba-diving trip
To find the hidden treasure ship.

So I find the ship below,
Down into the hold I go,
There's treasure there for me to spend . . .
                              But none to lend!

Andrew McBlain (10)
Ballyvester Primary School

MY CAT

My cat is like a couch,
Gingery, soft and a big slouch
I picture my cat at night,
Out hunting in the garden.
He is like a banana
His tail is thin and bendy
He is a tropical tiger,
Striped and vicious.

Luke Summerville (11)
Ballyvester Primary School

CRAZY FOOTBALL

We all run onto the pitch,
In our shorts and stripes,
The ref runs onto the pitch in stitches,
The players are having a fight.

The ref blows his whistle,
And the game starts,
Number 4 gets hit by the ball,
And his leg smarts.

They play on grudgingly,
Because it starts to rain,
Someone gets a red card,
The ref is being a pain.

Number 3 scores a goal,
The crowd goes wild,
This puts the opposition ahead,
Oh! I wish I was in bed!

Sarah Ellis (10)
Crossgar Primary School

MOTOR SPORT

Cruising down the motorway
Racing the guy in front,
Just to speed him up a little
I give him a little shunt.

I can't wait until I get in the seat
It is the perfect place to be
I hope I pass my test
For that I'll have to strive.

Maybe I'll get a motorbike
That would be cool too
Going down the motorway
On two wheels, not four.

Stuart Orr (9)
Crossgar Primary School

MR BEAN

Mr Bean, he makes me laugh,
He really has no fear
Except for losing his teddy bear
The little bear with only one ear.

Mr Bean drives like mad,
Brmm! Brmm! Brmm! His Mini goes
I giggle and roar when he drives so bad
It even makes the policeman sad.

One day he went onto the beach
He was going for a swim
As he was changing into swimming trunks
He saw a man looking at him.
Mr Bean got very bashful
He did not know what to do
He did not want to change in public view.

Oh such a giggle it was to see the antics of Mr Bean
But what Mr Bean didn't know was that the man
        watching him was blind and could not even see.

Mr Bean is such a funny man
I'm his number one fan
My school pals laugh when I act his ways
It always brightens up their days.

Jonathan Woods (8)
Crossgar Primary School

KANGAROOS

Kangaroos are friendly
Fun to play with.
I love them.
I wish I had one.
They have babies
That live in a pouch
They come from Australia.

Christopher Broome (9)
Crossgar Primary School

ABOUT SCHOOL

I go to school to learn to read
And count and write.
I go to school to see my friends.
Back home at night
I do some work.
I get it right.
I love school.

Cherilyn Hasley (8)
Crossgar Primary School

FISH

I like to fish
And I wish
I could fish
All day long
And sing a song.
Oh I wish
I could fish.

Daryl Hasley (9)
Crossgar Primary School

SCHOOL

It's break time and I have to stay inside,
I have a rhyme to do,
The teacher calls me over,
She says, 'Go outside, don't be so blue.'

The children play football and hide-and-seek,
We all play together and have lots of fun,
John kicks the ball,
To see how fast I can run.

Now break time is over,
All the crisps have been eaten,
And the lemonade's gone,
We go back inside for music and song.

It's not long till home time,
It's been a good day,
There goes the bell,
Hip hip hooray!

Caolán Heath (8)
Crossgar Primary School

LIONS

Lions live in a large family group
They live in Africa
And parts of India
Where it is very hot.
Babies are called cubs.
I like going to the zoo
To see all the lions.

Victoria Jamison (8)
Crossgar Primary School

MY BEST FRIEND

My best friend, her name is Grace,
And she has a really pretty face,
She has a very brilliant mind,
And she is one of a kind,
She always gives, she also shares,
If something's wrong, she always cares,
She is extra smart,
And she's great at art,
She is really trusting,
And she is helping,
If I need her, I shout 'Grace' and I click,
And she'll be there extra quick,
She is funny and she is fun,
And she is as bright as the sun.

Anneke Taylor (9)
Crossgar Primary School

THE BEACH

The beach is full of fun things and I jump up like a jelly pie.
I go over to the rock pools where I fish for crabs,
Starfish and little sea snails
I am happy on the beach because
I have so much fun
I play hide-and-seek on the sand dunes with my friends
The dunes are both big and small
And some are very tall.
I have a donkey ride and buy ice cream
Sometimes I fly my kite
The wind can be strong and it blows my kite
Up, up and away.

Joe McKinney (8)
Crossgar Primary School

THE SEASONS

Spring has arrived
Everything is so bright.
Lambs are being born
It's a wonderful sight.

Summer is here,
I'm full of good cheer.
This is my favourite
Time of the year.

Autumn has come
The trees are getting bare.
Leaves are lying on the ground
Lots of colour around.

Winter is upon us
Snow is falling down.
We are building a snowman
So we can knock him down.

Jason Gallagher (8)
Crossgar Primary School

SCHOOL

From Monday to Friday,
Nine to three,
I go to school and learn my A, B, C,
Adding up, taking away,
Doing maths every day.
A tick here, and an 'X' there,
Boys in the playground pulling hair!

Deborah Lauren McSpadden (7)
Crossgar Primary School

OUR CARAVAN SITE

At our caravan site we have lots of fun,
We love to play in the sun,
We ride our bikes and swing on swings
And do lots and lots of different things.

We can go to the beach
Or go to the shop,
Swim in the pool
Or when it's really hot,
Dad will do a barbecue.

We eat sausages and drumsticks
Chicken and steak
And lots of salad that Mum can make
When we've finished our food
We go back to play - that is good!

Kenneth Campbell (9)
Crossgar Primary School

MY CAT TIGGER

My cat Tigger is fat and lazy,
He never chases a mouse,
He hides on me, and then jumps out,
He purrs and purrs all day long,
He's tabby and furry, silly and mad,
He's always hungry,
He's the best cat in the world,
One day when I went to get in the car,
I heard a funny sound, then I saw my cat,
With a tin over his head,
My cat Tigger is really silly,
But really bad.

Christine Nelson (8)
Crossgar Primary School

MEMORIES OF MEG

Meg was my dog,
She was eighteen years old,
She was playful and cute,
But sometimes was bold.
She loved to be stroked,
Or be given a cuddle,
And then she'd run off,
And jump in a puddle!
She was always so happy,
And ready for fun,
And liked nothing better,
Than to go for a run.
I miss her now when she's not here,
But my memories of Meg, I hold very dear.

Rachel Campbell (9)
Crossgar Primary School

MY DOG MEG

My dog Meg is very funny,
She jumps on me and hurts my tummy,
She is white and brown and full of fun,
She likes to play and run and run,
Her hair is shaggy and very long,
I chase her and she jumps about,
She comes into the house and Mum says
'Get out.'
I love Meg, the way she is clever,
And I'll love her for ever and ever.

Ashleigh Buttle (8)
Crossgar Primary School

THE TITANIC

The Titanic was a great ship,
That sailed across the sea.
Belfast to Southampton,
Then to Cherbourg in Normandy.

After Cherbourg she travelled to
Queenstown in Ireland,
To pick up more passengers,
Like me and you.

The Titanic started sailing,
In all its splendour
Right across the Atlantic,
Trying to get to New York.

But sadly she struck an iceberg,
'Oh no!' the captain said,
Then she split in two,
And sank to the seabed.

Lauren Hamilton (11)
Crossgar Primary School

THE SEA

I went to the sea
To paddle my feet
I went right into the shiny bit
It was only me and the big, big sea.
I splashed and I laughed
When the sand slid through my feet
It was time to go but
I had fun in the big, big sea.

Natalie Murphy (8)
Crossgar Primary School

SPRING AND SUMMER

Spring

Springtime is upon us,
And new life has begun,
Little lambs are leaping,
And playing in the sun.

Flowers are now unfolding,
The sun is shining high,
And all the little birdies,
Are flying in the sky.

Summer

The sun is getting hotter,
It's time to laugh and play,
Children, excited and happy,
Looking forward to every day.

Families are packing their cases,
It's time to get on the plane,
Sun, sea, swimming and sandcastles,
We're off on our holidays again.

Susan Coulter (8)
Crossgar Primary School

DECORATING THE CHRISTMAS TREE

Decorating the Christmas tree is a lot of fun,
Getting Rudolph a carrot and Santa, milk and a bun.
Down the chimney he comes,
And then they fill their tums
And in my bed, there I lie,
Waiting to eat a nice mince pie.

Christopher Taylor (7)
Crossgar Primary School

MY QUAD

My quad, it does go flying
I always win the race
It throws up a lot of mud
It always splats about my face.
Then all you hear is
'Don't go so fast, slow down!'
Then it's time to have a race
But just guess who wins?
Yes, it's me again!
But now it's time to put her in,
Next morning out she comes.
She flies about.
The best quad gets the prize
Oh yes, I've won!
I put the medal on the fireplace and smile.

Jonathan Buttle (10)
Crossgar Primary School

MY ALIEN FRIEND

My alien's been with me for two years,
He's got four eyes and very big ears.
He came to Earth, he has a rocket;
He took me to space to see the comet.
He has a green body, and a funny green face.
Oh, by the way, his name is Ace!
Ace is my friend, he's really fun,
He's been to the moon' he's been to the sun.
He talks like a baby, but I don't care.
He also has funny purple hair!

John Emerson (8)
Crossgar Primary School

MY KART

I have a kart, it is so cool,
It would make spectators stand and drool,
Off I go like a raging bull,
When it comes to karting, I'm no fool.
Faster and faster, this is brill,
But round the bends are better still.
This is where I show my skill
Passing people at my will.
Bump! Crash! I've had a crash,
Nothing bad but I had a dash.
Never mind, it happens, they say,
I'll be back another day.

David Bell (9)
Crossgar Primary School

MY FRIENDS

My friends are very good
But not always in a nice mood.
In the playground we play
Always having fun each day.
In the class we work hard *(not)*.

Tomorrow is another day
Waiting for my friends to come and play.
In the playground we have fun
Dancing around in the sun.
Together we say, 'Goodbye.'
Till another day comes around.

April Jamison (10)
Crossgar Primary School

SISTERS

Little sister, big sister
Sometimes fighting over toys.
We laugh and play together,
Though never with the boys.

Sharing make-up secrets
Telling stories in the dark
If we're not on the PlayStation,
We're riding bikes in the park.

It doesn't matter how often we argue,
We still love one another
Cos we're more than friends, you see,
We're sisters.

Natalie McSpadden (9)
Crossgar Primary School

A BEST FRIEND

Best friend, best friend,
Everyone needs a best friend,
Someone to play with,
Share secrets with.

You can have more than one friend
But can only have one best friend.
You may play with a group of friends
But only one of them is your best friend.

When you have a best friend
You can trust them not to tell a secret.
But a friend could tell a secret.
Do you have a best friend?

Sharon McCorkell (11)
Crossgar Primary School

MR SNOWMAN

One morning it started snowing.
My face was all a-glowing.
I wrapped up all cosy and warm.
A day in the snow would do me no harm.
I went outside and had lots of fun,
But I could not find the sun.
I found a bucket and a spade,
Soon a snowman I had made.
I found a hat to put on his head,
Boy, my fingers were going dead!
I looked for a carrot to use as a nose,
Now I can barely feel my toes.
For his eyes I'll need some coal,
Isn't he a cold old soul?
My nose is rather cold and red,
I think I'll call my snowman, Fred.

Grace Emerson (10)
Crossgar Primary School

RED IS ...

Red is a clown's nose, funny and big.
Red is the colour of my favourite team.
Red is the colour of my school uniform.

Red is a flame, burning bright.
Red at night is a shepherd's delight.
Red is the colour of Santa's suit.
Red is the colour of my favourite car.

Loren McNeely (9)
Crossgar Primary School

CHAT

Girls chat about pop stars,
Which band is going to be No 1,
Who's going to win Pop Idol,
About the Brit Awards and how well
                    they have done.

Girls chat about clothes,
The latest fashion,
What new tops and trousers we have,
And which are designer and which are cons.

Girls chat all the time,
They just want to have fun,
Go shopping and play games,
And drink Coke in the sun.

Rebecca Orr (11)
Crossgar Primary School

MY DOG

My dog is called Trooper
He barks all day long,
He loves to chase birds
He's so very strong.

He has long, wiry hair
All tangled and twisted,
It gets brushed once or twice,
It desperately needs it.

I really like my dog Trooper
He really is so super.
He is my friend, who's always there,
With his long and tangly hair.

Hannah Cuffey (9)
Crossgar Primary School

THE WIND

Oh wind you blow, you blow so hard
You knock me clean off my guard
Your blustery gust knocked off my gate
My dad says the bolts were on too late

You puff and blast causing a storm
Making waves crash in very bad form
You roar and whistle in the night
I shiver and shake in a fright

While I try to sleep in bed alone
I listen for the familiar drone
Of my dad snoring and breathing deeply
But your deafening wind makes it all
So creepy.

Niamh Gilgunn (8)
Drumaness Primary School

WIND

Oh wind, oh wind how long you stay
It seems you have been here many a day.
The way you go over the sea
Making waves on your journey
Across the grass and against the trees.
Where are you going in such a hurry?
You blow away everything in your way.
You blow the houses off their sockets.
Show yourself!

Jamie Dougherty (8)
Drumaness Primary School

WIND

Wind, oh wind, heavy or light,
You always stay in a place of fright,

In a breeze or in a storm,
Every time a different form,

Wind, you're calm but strong,
How do you set off a gong?

No animal including a boar,
Can compare to your mighty roar,

Don't you know you can tame
Even the strongest flame?

You can blow a raging river,
You can make anyone shiver.

Patrick Gartland (9)
Drumaness Primary School

THE WIND

The wind blows high as the days go by
I saw you taking my kite
Doing robbery in daylight
Why can't I see you?
I just walk around the corner and you are in my face.
Rain, hail, sleet or snow.
It all seems worse when the wind starts to blow.

Michelle O'Hare (9)
Drumaness Primary School

NIGHT

Night is my kind and loving grandma.
She comforts me in my time of need.

She is very graceful and silent and sometimes makes me feel lonely.
She is full of peaceful and tranquil sounds and smells very fragrant.

She has a comforting and twilight face.
Her eyes are glittering blue and twinkling in the darkness.

She is wearing pale red lipstick and has a very comforting smile.
Her hair is long blonde and tied in a ribbon.

She is wearing also a long white robe and a pair of sandals.

She moves both swiftly and slowly along the thick clouds in the sky
And then suddenly she disappears behind the clouds
To her castle where she lives.

My dear grandma hypnotises me in the darkness of her eyes.

Fiona Oldroyd (11)
Drumaness Primary School

NIGHT

Night is spooky.
He makes me feel insecure.
His face looks bad, his eyes are dark red.
His mouth is big and wide.
His hair is black and shaggy.
His clothes are made of black silk.
When he moves, he sounds like thunder.
When he speaks it sounds evil.
He lives in a haunted house with blood and bodies.
Night terrifies me.

Rachel McCaugherty (10)
Drumaness Primary School

NIGHT

Night is a nasty, bad burglar with a scary grin.
He has a way of making me feel insecure
And gives me nightmares and makes me feel creepy.
I get the shivers when I think of him.
Most people say he's nice, but not me.
His eyes are green and brown.
His hair is dark and black.
His mouth is big and wide.
His clothes are black and creepy.
He moves quickly.
He might even come from space.
When he comes I hide under the bed covers.

Emma Rice (10)
Drumaness Primary School

ONOMATOPOEIA POEM

Vroom!
The car goes racing by
Splash!
The rain comes from the sky
Groan!
When I cut my knee
Shuffle!
When I'm on the settee
Rattle!
Goes the knife and fork
Pop!
Went the Champagne cork.

Laura Mason (11)
Drumaness Primary School

ONOMATOPOEIA POEM

Shuffle
When I deal out the cards.

Buzz
Buzz goes the bee that flies.

Creak
The sound of a rusty gate that can't open.

Lash
The lash of raindrops when it is a rainy day.

Hiss
The sound that a snake makes.

Boom
The bang of a bomb being exploded.

Nathan Madine (10)
Drumaness Primary School

THE WIND

Oh wind, oh wind, how strong you are.
I don't know who you are, at night you are so strange.
I still don't know who you are.
Oh wind, oh wind, you blow all day long.
It sounds like a song.
I saw the things you have done but you have hidden
away from me.
I heard you call me in the night.
The wind blows up in the high sky.

Hannah Bell (9)
Drumaness Primary School

ONOMATOPOEIA POEM

Plop!
The raindrops fall down

Jingle!
Santa Claus comes to town

Chug!
The car just won't start

Whee!
Going down a hill in a cart

Pop!
The balloon burst on a tree

Squeal!
Shouts Mum when she sees a mouse eating cheese.

Rachel Gallagher (10)
Drumaness Primary School

NIGHT

Night is kind and lovely and comforting.
A sweet dream is my present from him.
He is my caring grandpa.
I am safe because of him.

He has a nice face and a sparkly smile.
He moves slowly and lives in the sky.
He makes everything better.

Emma Marner (11)
Drumaness Primary School

THE ROBOT

Here comes the robot *bzz bzz crunch*
Fell off the wall and landed on his lunch.
Here comes the robot *bzz bzz creak*
Here comes the robot all this week.
Here comes the robot *bzz bzz thump*
Here comes the robot *bump bump bump.*

Eve McCartney (8)
Drumaness Primary School

WHAT AM I?

As fast as lightning,
Eyes like sparkling diamonds,
Cries like a baby most of the time,
It's as dark as the night sky,
It lives in foreign countries
It eats other animals.

Daniel Lennon (11)
Drumaness Primary School

WHAT AM I?

His feet are like flippers
His skin is like silk
He eats bread
He is fluffy like a fleece
He sleeps with his head under the water.

Michaela Boyd (11)
Drumaness Primary School

THE WIND

I think I saw you the other day
When I was outside to play
I thought I heard you howl
But did not know if you would growl.
I saw all the things you did
But you always seemed to hide
But never did I see you, kid.

Martin McAlister (8)
Drumaness Primary School

WHAT AM I?

It is said that witches use me,
I am as black as the night sky,
My eyes glow like the night lights,
When I'm happy I make a noise like your tummy,
My skin is soft as a cushion
And my tail is all bushy like a bunch of leaves.

Rebecca Robinson (11)
Drumaness Primary School

UGLY SISTER

I have an ugly young sister.
One day she gave me a blister.
It was so very sore,
I think she's a bore
And I hope she's blown in a twister.

Lisa Ferris (11)
Drumaness Primary School

VOLCANOES

The explosions are loud,
There is a big crowd.
Running in the street,
I fell from my feet.

The boulders are flying,
The people are crying.
The trees are on fire,
Volcanoes getting higher.

The lava is plopping,
There is no stopping.
The smoke is in the air,
The people are in despair.

Lava is hissing,
Can't stop missing.
My home's burnt to the ground,
I'm running all around.

The volcano is my enemy,
It is always going to get me.
The ash is on the ground,
The volcano's cooling down

A sense of relief,
The volcano went to sleep.
I cry and weep,
In my sleep.

Philip Cochrane (10)
Fairhill Primary School

A River Of Glowing Flame

The Earth is cracking open,
And there's screaming all around.
Smoke is commencing,
I hear a bubbling sound.

The lava is coming down,
Like a stream of glowing light.
I dread to see again,
On this fearful night.

The villagers fleeing,
From their burning homes.
I am running too
As the lava roams.

The volcano spits exploding rock,
As well as clouds of smoke.
I smell various gases,
And I'm beginning to choke.

The volcano lies dormant,
In the sunny sky.
It is a beautiful sight,
As the birds fly by.

Jordan Brown (10)
Fairhill Primary School

Mum

Mum is a crimson red.
She is a soft sofa.
Mum is a sweet song.
She is a rug on a warm beach.

Mum is a snug coat.
She is a glass of lemonade in the sun.
Mum is a warm nuzzling dog.
She is a cosy winter fire.

Gareth Rowan (10)
Fairhill Primary School

AN ANGRY WORLD

The ground starts shaking,
Is this a volcano in the making?
A river of lava starts spewing out,
What have we done to deserve this plight?

The volcano grows firm and tall,
'Help us,' is the villagers' call,
A fiery lake comes flowing down,
Giant boulders smashing all around.

This cruel monster is growing tall,
Black raindrops of ash are starting to fall.
The mountain is blowing its top,
A mass of rocks are ready to drop.

This monstrous beast is still in wrath,
We have to get out of its cruel path.
There are dangerous gases in the air,
But this terrible monster does not care.

The molten lava is cooling down,
But there is little left of our town,
This monster is now sleeping
And we have memories we will be keeping.

Robin Harte (11)
Fairhill Primary School

VOLCANO

The noise is like thunder,
You hear it all around
And the feeling of rumbling,
Shaking on the ground.

Hot lava
Pouring down the side
And the people in the village
Running as they cried.

Exploding like fireworks,
Coming down with clouds of dust
And the village is left
With smoke and rust.

Now it is empty,
The people have gone.
The volcano is left
Singing a triumphant song.

The volcano is sleeping,
Finally, at last
The terrible hour
Is eventually past.

Nadine Lee Hamilton (11)
Fairhill Primary School

MY AUNT

My aunt is a lovely red,
She is a soft cosy bed,
My aunt is a loud whisper,
She is a way through a winter garden.

My aunt is a warm cosy scarf,
She is a hot cup of cocoa,
My aunt is a warm snoozing dog,
She is winter's snow.

Leah Ruth Redmond (9)
Fairhill Primary School

THE WORST NIGHTMARE

In a peaceful village
A man goes out to work.
A rumbling starts, then a crack
Red, glowing, spitting lava forms
A big explosion.
Red ribbons of glowing fire
Come floating down the side.
Smoke and gas are all we smell.
People dying a fiery death,
Our crops and houses covered in ash,
The sparks light the night.

Another crack and hissing starts
A crackle, plopping and roaring.
Another explosion, more lava
Comes flowing like a river,
The trees are burning,
People are dying and running
Screaming and shouting as the lava flows on.
Rocks are shooting like fireworks,
Then it dies down.
The lava cools, it looks like the moon,
People crying, their houses gone,
The village destroyed.
The monster sleeps.

Andrew McCammond (10)
Fairhill Primary School

THE FEARSOME FIRES OF RAGE

A cold, dark evening a crack appeared,
Everybody looked, the dogs flicked their ears,
People ran, birds took flight,
And it all took place that fateful night.

A mound appeared and rocks went crashing,
Massive mice they were smashing,
People screaming, running dogs,
Ash covered us like thick fog.

Al the lava's flowing and rushing,
Many people, rocks are crushing,
The volcano is a giant mountain,
Lava shoots out like a magma fountain.

People are fleeing right now,
They will come back some day, some how,
Everyone had a horrid fright,
Why did God give us this awful plight?

Samuel Gibson (11)
Fairhill Primary School

MY DOG

Bone chewer
Shoe eater
Mouse catcher
Flea scratcher
Cat chaser
Tail wagger.

Katie Hunter (10)
Fairhill Primary School

THE WORLD OF FLAMES

The volcano stands, proud and tall,
A rumble, a bang, and lava falls.
Rocks roll down, like an angry steam train,
The ash blankets light, a cloud of dark rain.

The people run screaming from the town,
Only one boat to safety, they all crowd round.
Explosions and screaming, these are the sounds,
And all this started, from a fissure in the ground.

The houses are burning,
There is acid in the lake,
I wish this would stop,
For everyone's sake.

The volcano stops, after hours of turmoil,
There is only ash, and not a trace of soil.
No crops and no buildings, and everyone flees,
But they will never forget
The wonders they've seen.

Elliot Russell (11)
Fairhill Primary School

MY COUSIN

My cousin is a rosy red
She's as soft as a sofa
My cousin is a gentle laugh
She is as bright as sunny Spain
My cousin is as warm as a blanket
She is a fuzzy rabbit
My cousin is as quick as a cat
She is the summer's sun.

Yasmin Orrell (10)
Fairhill Primary School

RIVER OF LAVA

A crack across the land,
Burst lava everywhere.
Clouds of ash drifting down like light snow,
People stampeding across the smoky lava land.

River of lava,
Burning sulphur and tree.
Grey powdery ash,
Clouds of smoke,
We can't even see.

Balls of rock in the air,
Like giant cannonballs,
Exploding everywhere.

It has gone cold as ice,
The volcano now dormant,
It is asleep again,
This terrible monster.

Rachel Blair (10)
Fairhill Primary School

DAD!

My dad is a crimson red
He is a comfy chair
He is very quiet
He is a place of winter snow
My dad is a T-shirt on a beach
He is as bitter as vinegar
He is like my black horse
He is the sun shining in the summer.

Lydia Brown (10)
Fairhill Primary School

THE FIERCE VOLCANO

A thick, red river of lava,
Spewing out of the fierce volcano,
Thick raindrops of rock are raining on the village,
Terrified people fleeing like a stampede.

Explosions and rumbling, crackling and banging,
Are the noises from the fierce volcano,
Some people are crying and others quite scared,
They know once the volcano stops
Everything will be ruined.

It starts to cool, but it still goes on,
The people are out and nowhere to be seen,
Eventually it calms and everything is bare,
Absolutely nothing left apart from thick ash layers.

Stephen Woods (10)
Fairhill Primary School

MUM!

Mum is like a sky blue.
She is a comfy and warm bed.
Mum, she can shout a lot
She is a Cyprus beach.
Mum is as warm as a big jacket.
She is like a warm cup of coffee at the fire
Mum is like an Arctic fox
She is summer and sun.

Leanne McCaughtry (10)
Fairhill Primary School

THE FEARSOME VOLCANO

A cold evening in 1997.
The ground started to shake
Like a pile of unsteady books.
Lava pouring out like a flowing river.
Rocks blasting out as fireworks.
Smoke spouting from the volcano chimney.
Ash floating down out of the sky.
Lava hissing as it flows into the river.
The lava glowing like a fearsome fire.
Trees and crops are crackling as they burn.
The volcano stops with a final rumble
As it cools and forms patterns.
Dormant.

Adam Drinkwater (10)
Fairhill Primary School

BROTHER!

My brother is like light green.
He is a really comfy chair.
My brother is a loud shouter.
He's a path through autumn.
My brother is a warm hat.
He is a drink by the fire.
My brother is a sleeping dog.
He is a summer sun.

Charmaine Kinkaid (10)
Fairhill Primary School

THE RIVER OF BLOOD

The volcano starts to erupt and everyone flees,
On a cold winter's night, the people are like bees.
Lava, a red ribbon of glowing fire,
Crack! The volcano goes, I hope it'll soon tire.
A gigantic fireworks display in the sky,
Only a dog has run by.
I can see more rocks crashing,
More and more are bashing
And the river is like blood,
We are having a lava flood.
All the houses go up in flames,
The volcano is the only one to blame.
Finally, the volcano is sleeping,
And everyone comes out, peeping.
I do not want to see that glowing, lava light,
Like on this terrible, fearful night.

Lucy McCausland (10)
Fairhill Primary School

MY MUM

My mum is a rosy red
She's like a comfy sofa
My mum has a soft whisper
She's as calm as a peaceful forest
My mum is as snug as a jumper
She loves to drink a cup of tea beside the cosy fire
My mum is a sleepy cat
She loves the summer sunshine.

Jonathan Robert Redmond (10)
Fairhill Primary School

THE BIG VOLCANO

It is a lovely day
Everybody is joyful and gay
Lots of people are running around
I hear a dreadful sound.

There are people screaming
The lava's like a waterfall streaming
A whole lot of people are dying
And most of us are crying.

The volcano's tummy is rumbling
And some people are tumbling
The lava is plopping
And we are not stopping.

We all go back
And there's a big crack
I will have to find a job
While all the people weep and sob.

Reece Boal (10)
Fairhill Primary School

MY BEST FRIEND

My best friend is bright yellow.
She is a hard cabin bed.
My best friend is a loud whisper.
She is as warm as the Mediterranean Sea.
My best friend is a soft coat.
She is a moist carrot.
My best friend is a soft pony.
She is summer sun.

Jordanne Boal (9)
Fairhill Primary School

THE MONSTER BREAKS OUT

There is a rumbling
The Earth shakes
Crack! Hiss! Bang!
The monster erupts
Shooting fireballs everywhere.

Alarmed! Terrified!
Fleeing for their lives.
Running! Pushing! Falling! Screaming!
Leaving their homes
For the monster to capture.

Black smouldering ash
Silence reigns
Smoke-filled air
Lava turned to hard rock.
People in despair and heartbroken
That their homes are destroyed.

The monster has gone to sleep.

Michael Redmond (10)
Fairhill Primary School

MY FRIEND

My friend
Ball kicker
Ankle hacker
Lolly licker
Fun maker
Happy friend.

Adam Wilson (10)
Fairhill Primary School

THE RIVER OF LAVA

One calm day,
Everything was silent,
The birds were singing in the trees.

Then there was a bang,
Like a firework,
People came out of their homes,
Like terrified animals,
There was a rumbling like a giant's tummy.
Then I saw red hot lava.

It is lying dormant,
But soon it will erupt again,
Showing its anger,
When it explodes again.

Clarissa Brown (11)
Fairhill Primary School

SNOW

One night the snow came,
But this time with shame.
It started to bang on the roof,
Sounding like an elephant's hoof.

I looked out the window and what did I see?
A great big elephant looking at me.
His face looked evil and his lips curved with laughter
And the exact look of him made me cold after.

I woke up and realised it was all a dream,
And I looked out the window and the snow had a gleam.
But then I burst out with laughter,
And guess who turned up after?

Kyla Herron (10)
Fairhill Primary School

SNOW IN DECEMBER

Sparkling white around the place,
No beating sun upon your face.
Over mountains it's knee high,
White as clouds in the sky.

In December snow falls,
Nice decorations in the halls.

Dancing to the Christmas songs,
Evening fires with coal in the tongs.
Choirs singing from door to door,
Exciting presents on the floor.
Many celebrate Christmas day,
Baby Jesus sleeping on the hay.
Each little stocking filled with toys,
Remember to be good little girls and boys.

Melanie Barlow (10)
Fairhill Primary School

CLOUDS

I wonder what makes the clouds move?
I wonder if clouds have feelings?
I wonder if they're happy or sad?
Are they good or are they bad?
I wonder if I sat on a cloud would I fall straight through?
I wonder if I touched a cloud would it jump at me and shout *boo?*
I wonder if I felt a cloud would it be wet or would it be dry?
Will I ever be friends with a cloud?
I will just have to wonder.

Debbie Johnston (10)
Fairhill Primary School

CLOUD

Wonder where they come from,
Wonder where they go,
Wonder what they're made of
And if they scream and shout.
Wonder if I could catch a cloud
Way up in the sky,
Wonder if I caught one
Could I have a ride?
Wonder if I stood
Upon a fluffy cloud
Wonder if I would stay up,
Or fall to the ground?
Wonder if they talk or mime,
Wonder do they laugh?
Wonder if I said this poem
Would all the clouds laugh?

Stephanie Louise Martin (10)
Fairhill Primary School

MY BEST BUDDY

My best buddy is a lively orange,
She is a stylish sofa,
My best buddy is such a chatterbox,
She is like a beach because it is the colour of her hair,
My best buddy is as fluffy as a rabbit,
She is like a piece of cheese,
My best buddy is like a jumping kangaroo,
She is like a shining sun,
My best buddy.

Kathryn Chambers (9)
Fairhill Primary School

ERUPTION DAY

The ash is falling heavily,
Everyone everywhere is running,
Al the cars have started crashing,
As the ground has started splitting.

The lava starts pumping out,
Down the volcano like a river,
And when every boulder hits the ground,
The Earth gives a vicious quiver.

The boulders are the size of cars,
Shattering as they fall,
And anyone they explode near,
Lets out a frightening yell.

James Jess (10)
Fairhill Primary School

THE CORNER BOY

The corner boy was a little small,
His mummy owned a corner stall.
The corner boy always sat in the corner,
He looked like Little Jack Horner.

The corner boy was very shy,
He always wanted to fly.
The corner boy was very old,
He was nearly as old as his little foal.

The corner boy liked white fluffy clouds,
Especially when they were bunched in crowds.
The corner boy had an imaginary friend,
Who drove his mum round the bend.

Christopher McCandless (9)
Fairhill Primary School

MANIC PANIC

We lived at the foot of a volcano,
But on one day it exploded.
There were people running, stampeding down the hill,
I ran too, the mill was on fire,
I heard the gases, people screaming too.

I looked back around, all the slow runners die,
I'm going fast, I hope I don't have to say goodbye!
Rocks are flying like fireworks,
The river of lava is getting faster and faster.
More people are suffering and houses too.

All the lava is cooling like the face of the moon,
It is going as black as coal.
The volcano is dormant,
But it left a destructive path from that eruption.

Cameron McDougall (10)
Fairhill Primary School

MUM

Mum is an outstanding royal blue,
She is as soft and gentle like a pillow,
Mum's voice is a soft, warm echo,
She is a stream flowing through a meadow,
Mum is a warm blanket, which wraps you up when you're sad,
She is a soothing drink that helps you sleep,
Mum is like a playful little kitten,
She is the springtime sun to melt the snow.

Tamah Katy McMillan (10)
Fairhill Primary School

THE DISASTER

The chilling news of the disaster,
had struck the freezing Atlantic Ocean.

As a massive iceberg had
disturbed the peace and band of the Titanic.

Piercing the night are the screams of
babies crying and little children that are lost.

Large lifeboats less than half full
rowing away into the dark night sky.

Brave women having to leave their sons,
and to start a new life without them.

The tragic, expensive ship was about
To *sink!*

Gemma Kirvell (10)
Holywood Primary School

A NIGHT TO REMEMBER

It was a night to remember
It was so cold like December!
I seemed to be in that lifeboat forever
No one to come and rescue us,
Never before had I seen such terror!
More and more people jumping from the decks
Soon Titanic was such a wreck!
It was sinking down down!
Now there are people who had such a fright!
All in all it was one terrible night!

Sophie Cann (11)
Holywood Primary School

FAREWELL TITANIC

Passengers awaking from their nice warm beds,
Confusion and fear running through their heads.

What is this panic that has suddenly arose?
What is this water beneath my toes?

Rushing up onto the deck,
Captain coming up to check.

Questions asked, no answers found,
No one now is sleeping sound.

Shadows now rising high above,
Couples are giving their very last love.

Titanic now in a slope,
Crewmembers frantically giving up hope.

Gentlemen dressed up in their best,
Waving farewell to all the rest.

For they know they're going to die,
Kisses and hugs to say goodbye.

Rachael Gordon (11)
Holywood Primary School

TITANIC SINKS!

Iceberg *iceberg!* Hit the deck!
It might turn us into a wreck!

Oh no! screamed the crew,
This will never do!

We will never survive,
This ship is buzzing like a beehive!

The lifeboats women and children first,
No more in this one, it will burst!

The stern rose high,
In the midnight sky.

At two-thirty am
You could hear the screams of women, children and men.

Philippa Ramsay-Baggs (11)
Holywood Primary School

AN EPIC BATTLE

Tears stroke the window glass
Falling ever heavy
For clouds fill the air
And shade the world from hope

As darkness fell
Despair ruled the sky and sea
Shadows roamed high and low
And creatures were loose again

Lightning flashed
And light spread
Evil and good fought
The never-ending battle

Light prevailed
And spread once more
Golden glow in every corner
And darkness turned and fled.

Victoria S Magill (11)
Holywood Primary School

TITANIC GOES DOWN!

Suddenly the ship shook,
All the people went to look.

Such a glamorous ship,
That crashed down bit by bit!

All the people took fright, screaming
And panicking in the night.

But the orchestra continued to play
Even though they were going to stay.

Two hours later the ship cracked by
That time the lifeboats were nearly packed.

Women and children first they'd say,
As the orchestra started to play.

Then the ship went slowly down
Leaving all those behind to drown!

Katie Stevenson (11)
Holywood Primary School

THE UNSINKABLE SINKING

Here I am sitting on a lifeboat
And slowly the Titanic starts to slope.
Men start to yell and make a huge panic,
Women start to scream aboard the Titanic.

Here I am watching it all
As the ship cracks in half and people start to fall
Into the water that's freezing cold.
To get out of that people would pay gold.

Now there isn't any Titanic.
The people are dead, there's no sound of panic.
Here comes the Carpathia to save the surviving rest.
They weren't on time but they did their best.

Stephen McClenahan (10)
Holywood Primary School

A DREAM ENGRAVED IN GOLD

In Southampton and there she was,
A queen of hope and golden dreams.
Inside was nothing but paradise,
Floating upon a glistening sea.

The sweet sound of blissful music,
As happiness grows nearer.
She looks so proud but yet so gentle
When the crowd starts to cheer her.

Everything you see and hear
Gives you a different sensation
Some joy, some importance,
Some pride, some relaxation.

She towers over everyone
As her funnels gleam.
At last she starts to cruise along,
Titanic, the ship of dreams.

Victoria Mason (11)
Holywood Primary School

INTO THE DEN

They thought she was invincible,
The size of the ship was unbelievable.

It was a floating palace,
The giant dome was made of glass.

It set sail many years ago,
Into the sea's mighty flow.

It sliced through the waves like a knife,
But for that it lost sixteen hundred people's lives.

The captain of the ship had set it too fast,
They didn't turn in time to dodge the iceberg that looked like glass.

'Danger! Danger!' shouted the crew, 'Uncover the lifeboats!'
All the people watched, whoa how it floats.

'Women and children first' said the crew,
The man said, 'I'll pay you quite a few.'

Down go the lifeboats into the flow,
It's time to go.

The men said, 'We'll go down like gentlemen,
To our final resting, gentle den.'

Aaron Matthews (11)
Holywood Primary School

TITANIC'S TALE OF TRAGEDY

On April tenth, nineteen twelve
Titanic set its sail,
It left Southampton harbour
This is the tragic tale.

The band was playing upon the deck
While people came on board,
Some of them were famous,
Some were ladies, gents and lords.

The first class settled in,
So did the second and the third
They weren't allowed to see each other,
Well, that is what I heard.

Four happy days went past
All with luxury,
Until the night of the sinking
Soon they would all be in the sea.

The ship it struck an iceberg
Hidden in the tide,
The tip was barely seen in time
As it ripped Titanic's side.

The travellers ran for lifeboats
And some of the lives were saved,
But most were lost within the ship
Deep below the waves.

Jordan Adair (10)
Holywood Primary School

TITANIC DISASTER

Sailing along on the freezing cold sea,
All is quiet, passengers having tea.
When a mighty rumble came from starboard side,
Then came the sound of the gushing tide.

The passengers gathered in a crowd,
They all began to cry aloud.
'Save us from the freezing sea,
Help! Help! Please save me!'

One by one they boarded lifeboats,
Some were not even wearing coats.
The Titanic sank beneath the waves,
No more passengers could be saved.

Kerrie Majury (11)
Holywood Primary School

MY BABY BROTHER

In front of the Christmas tree,
I held my happy baby brother,
Sucking his thumb.

Mum said 'Don't drop him
He's very delicate.'

When the photo was taken
The baby cried and got his bottle.

When he calmed down
Another photo was taken.
Mum framed it and hung it on the wall.

Andrew Brontë (8)
Iveagh Primary School

As

As rough as a nettle, as smooth as a stone
As thin as a line, as flat as a phone
As old as a dog, as young as a baby
As short as a rat, as long as a ruby
As dirty as a bridge, as clean as a frown
As short as a finger, as long as a town
As slow as a tortoise, as fast as a hare
As evil as a witch, as nice as a teddy bear
As tall as a giraffe, as short as a lead
As neat as a picture, as un-neat as a bed
As fun as a game, as boring as a walk
As cold as in winter, as warm as a talk
As up as a cloud, as down as a sea
As square as a flag, as round as a pea
As jagged as a leaf, as toothed as a chip.

April Niblock (9)
Iveagh Primary School

My Baby Brother

Outside my house
I held my smiling baby brother.

Mum said 'Smile and don't drop him.'
He was small and delicate.

I felt happy and
I felt responsible and nervous.

Matthew Loughlin (9)
Iveagh Primary School

A RECIPE FOR CHRISTMAS

Pour a ladle of stars in a bowl, for Santa Claus.
Collect a bowl of wisemen, put them in a song.
Squeeze a dash of weddings, with a bit of confetti.
Mend an elf to help Santa to bring our presents.
Season snow, Santa's here, with a cup of tea for Mum.
Cover a tablespoon with tinsel, to Christmas carol away.
Mix a bowl of silver and gold sprinkles for people's homes.
Crunch a Christmas story, with a glass of magic in the snow.
Take an angel on a Christmas tree, to make it pretty for me.
Compound a poor snowman in the frost, melting, melting, melting.
Sprinkle turkey and ham, on a scrumptious meal and a mix of holly.
Pour a few crackers on a candle light in the wind.
Cut carefully Christmas cards all the way around the doors.

Gemma Davenport (9)
Iveagh Primary School

AS . . .

As yellow as a melon, as pink as a pig,
As dark as a hole, as light as a wig,
As hard as a rock, as soft as a pancake,
As shiny as silver, as dull as a black lake,
As long as a ruler, as short as a baby's finger,
As round as an apple, as brown as ginger,
As strong as a steel bar, as weak as a kitten,
As rough as a tree trunk, as soft as a mitten,

As wriggly as a snake, as slimy as a slug,
As hungry as a fox, as rough as a rug,
As nice as a friend, as bad as the Devil,
As ugly as a witch, as lovely as Revels,
As cunning as a fox, as poorly as a sick dog,
As light as a leaf, as grey as a hog,
As sweet as a pear, as bitter as a bad grape,
As thick as a brick, as noisy as a drum.

Amanda Johnston (10)
Iveagh Primary School

SADNESS/HAPPINESS

Sadness

Sadness is jet-black
It smells like sunlight
It tastes like blue, mouldy sandwiches
It sounds like sick Titanic music
It feels like burnt grass
And lives in the wind.

Happiness

Happiness is mint green
It smells like roses in the garden
It tastes like meatballs
It sounds like Steps
It feels like sunburn
And lives in the sun.

Jeffrey McNeilly (10)
Iveagh Primary School

LOVE AND HATRED

Love

Love is a crimson red
It tastes like sweet jelly
It smells like fresh roses in the garden
Love looks like a rosy pair of cheeks
And sounds like sugar pouring over cereal
Love is warm and cosy.

Hatred

Hatred is a dull grey
It tastes like sour milk
It smells like old chicken
Hatred looks like a damp paper bag
It sounds like smashing glass
Hatred is ugly and bad.

Ryan Weir (10)
Iveagh Primary School

HAPPINESS AND SADNESS

Happiness

Happiness is baby blue
And smells like pies sitting in a window
Happiness tastes like Pepsi
And sounds like birds in the baby blue sky
Happiness feels like you've got something you've always wanted
And it lives in your heart.

Sadness

Sadness is dull black
And smells like sour milk
Sadness tastes like grass
And sounds like guns going off
Sadness feels like someone took things you've always wanted
And lives in the ground.

Andrew Magill (10)
Iveagh Primary School

WAR AND PEACE

War

War is red
It tastes like burnt potatoes
It smells like smoke from a fire
War looks like the rubble from a broken-down house
It sounds like a Jackhammer on concrete
War feels like the hottest water in the world against bare skin.

Peace

Peace is turquoise
It tastes like sugar and icing
Peace smells like perfume
It looks like a wedding cake
It sounds like ballerina music
Peace feels happy and soft.

Steven Rowland (10)
Iveagh Primary School

WAR AND PEACE

War

War is ruby red
It smells like uncooked fish sitting in the sink
And tastes like a very hot curry
War sounds like a squeaky door
It feels spiky and painful
War lives in the desert.

Peace

Peace is turquoise
It smells like freshly cut grass in the morning
And it tastes like newly baked bread
Peace sounds like the wind
It feels like a warm bath
Peace lives in the golden sun.

Jonathan Graham (9)
Iveagh Primary School

MY BABY BROTHER

My baby brother is so tiny
He feels like a soft teddy bear

He's so cute and he's small
He's like a sleepy ball.
When I was in the park he wet himself.

When my mum said
'Are you ready?' I said, 'Yes'
She took a photograph and then he cried.

Laura-Mae Johnston (8)
Iveagh Primary School

JOY AND FEAR

Joy

Joy is lilac
It smells like a red rose given to you by your boyfriend
It tastes like strawberries and cream
Joy sounds like an orchestra playing 'The Four Seasons' composed
by Vivaldi
It feels like your fluffy pet rabbit
Joy lives in the gold streets of heaven.

Fear

Fear is raven
It smells like a forest fire in the middle of summer
It tastes like burnt toast
Fear sounds like a cannon going off
It feels like sandpaper that hasn't been used
Fear lives in the fires of Hell.

Hannah McKnight (10)
Iveagh Primary School

MY BABY BROTHER

My baby brother is as soft as a teddy bear.
He looks cute and tiny as can be.

Grannie put him on my lap and told me to smile.
I felt grown up. He felt delicate.

We took the photo out in the garden.
It was lovely.

Samantha McCartney (8)
Iveagh Primary School

UP IN THE ATTIC, DOWN IN THE CELLAR

(And something's . . . rustling)
Plastered pictures
Tattered tricycle
Broken basket
Trashed toys
Rusty record players
Scruffy schoolbooks
Up in the attic

Down in the cellar . . .
Creaking cooker
Dirty dishes
Some woodwormy woodwork
Frozen freezers
Broken bathtub
Tatty toolbox
(And something's . . . screaming!)

Keely Dougan (10)
Iveagh Primary School

MY BABY BROTHER

I was very proud holding my new baby brother in the hospital.
He was light and very small and cosy like a teddy bear.

I was very nervous in case I dropped him, he cried a lot.
When he was coming home he had to be well wrapped up
Because it was cold outside.

When we got home Dad took a picture
Of me and my new baby brother.
When Dad took the photo he cried.

Sara Dougan (8)
Iveagh Primary School

Joy And Sadness

Joy

Joy is sky-blue
It smells like fresh grass
Joy tastes like an apple
It sounds like pop stars singing
It feels like a leaf
Joy lives in your heart.

Sadness

Sadness is jet-black
It smells like a mucky puppy
And tastes like a solid potato
Sadness sounds like a sad song
It feels like the rough bark of a tree
It lives in the devil.

Tiffany Williams (9)
Iveagh Primary School

A Recipe For Christmas

Gather two cups of pudding then a cup of sweets
Add an ounce of angels, some snow and Santa
Collect a pack of cards and some shining stars
Pour holly and ivy and some mince pies and ham
Squeeze some orange for a cake and some carol singers
Stir in mistletoe and some presents
Season with Christmas trees
Mix crackers and holidays and Mary and Joseph.

Jonathan Bready (10)
Iveagh Primary School

Up In The Attic, Down In The Cellar

(and . . . something's . . . crawling)
sad rocking horse
aged pictures
old birthday cards
cobwebby Christmas tree
scruffy schoolbooks
old gramophones
Up in the attic . . .

Down in the cellar . . .
rusty mousetraps
antique bike
damp newspapers
rusty cooker
scruffy suitcases
aged washing machine
(and . . . something's . . . smelling!)

Jamie Wright (10)
Iveagh Primary School

The Old Tree

The leaves are as green as grass on the old tree
Later the leaves turn orange and yellow like the sun
Soon the branches are as brown as chocolate
The tree now is as high as the sky and the bark is as rough as the ground
The fruit now is as red as a pepper
The seeds are as tiny as millions
Later the flowers are as small as a seed.

Leah Shilliday (9)
Iveagh Primary School

A RECIPE FOR CHRISTMAS

Take a dash of snow, add a bit of Jesus
Knead a bit of the nativity
Mix a glass of Schloer
Squeeze a cup of holly
Imagine a packet of presents
Blend an ounce of angels
Stand by for Santa
Gather a bowl of stars
Empty your decorations out
Put up your Christmas tree
Go quietly because Jesus is born
Call over a couple of friends
Season it by adding Mary
Cover it with a tablespoon of ivy
Begin it again next year.

Laura Phillips (9)
Iveagh Primary School

A NEW LIFE

When we came home from church
I got into my jeans and ran down the hall,
Mum said to me 'I want a photo.'

I sat on the settee,
Mum gave her to me,
She wriggled and squiggled
As she sat on my knee.

I do love her you know,
In a special sort of way,
She is my sister.

Heather Bell (9)
Iveagh Primary School

MY SMALL CUDDLY BROTHER

My baby brother and I got a photograph
Taken at my own house.
He was very small and he felt cuddly
Like my best teddy bear.

I was scared in case I dropped him.
He cried very loudly all the time
When his dummy fell out of his mouth.
He was three months old.

Matthew King (9)
Iveagh Primary School

MY BABY SISTER

When she cries she is like a miniature twister.
She has more hair than Mr Vance and
When she is sleeping she is like a teddy bear.
When she is getting a photograph taken
She sometimes smiles and sometimes cries.

Gareth Wilson (9)
Iveagh Primary School

MY BABY BROTHER

My baby brother is cute, he is bald, we got our photo taken.
I liked that day we got our photo taken at the seaside.
It was a nice sunny day.
When I was holding the baby I felt responsible and scared
But he was happy.

Robert Bell
Iveagh Primary School

My Baby Brother

My baby brother and I,
Got a photo taken at the zoo,
He didn't give a wiggle,
Until he heard a 'moo'!

He cried and cried,
All night and day,
My mother said,
'Get him out of the way!'

Holly Mitchell (9)
Iveagh Primary School

As . . .

As dumb as a dog, as smart as a cat,
As rich as a king, as poor as a rat,
As young as a baby, as old as a house,
As thick as a tree, as thin as a mouse,
As long as a post, as short as a stick,
As big as a tree, as small as a tick.

Aaron Megaw (10)
Iveagh Primary School

My Baby Sister

My little sister was nice and warm when I held her.
She felt heavy to me but she was cuddly.
She looked cute and tiny and she was happy.
I felt grown up, I felt delighted and responsible.
The photo was taken at the hotel and it was great fun.

Jenny Waddell (8)
Iveagh Primary School

UP IN THE ATTIC (AND SOMETHING'S CREAKING)

Scruffy, school books
Old pictures of pies
Musty clown clothes
Broken, brown basket
Rich rocking horse
Grubby gramophone
Up in the attic.

Down in the cellar . . .
Black, bold writing on wall
Costly china vase
Old posters of animals
Smells from piles of socks
Cracked, clockwork mouse
Rough record player
(And something's running . . .).

Emma Jayne Johnston (10)
Iveagh Primary School

UNDER THE SEA

Under the sea is a sunken ship
Which I am going to see
It might be fake or it might be true
But to see it is something I must do
An octopus thief is on my tail
But I am an expert thief and I cannot fail
I got there before the thief
So I took the golden rings and the crown
And swam very quickly.

Ryan Wilkinson (8)
Killyleagh Primary School

CLEOPATRA THE GODDESS QUEEN

Cleopatra the goddess queen
With her treasures that people
Might have seen
Cleopatra the goddess queen.

Tutankhamun her pharaoh chum
He killed Howard Carter
But he was the best
He should be happy not glum.

Look at the treasures
They were so attractive
I wonder if they decorated the mice.

But I've had to be
Buried with all my treasures
To rest till the afterlife.

Adam McClurg (9)
Killyleagh Primary School

OWLS

Owls swooping quietly across the rooftops
Hooting in the moonlight
Silent, flying to prey
Giant eyes looking down
Tearing prey apart with their sharp claws
Stretching their long legs
Fluttering like a butterfly
The night shift bird flying everywhere
Barn owl, white and beautiful.

Amber Marks (8)
Killyleagh Primary School

MY SCHOOL BAG

In
My bag
There's probably
A packet of
Gum for all
I know there's
Probably ten
Books or
Homework
Not done or
A note for
Home or some
Pens so in my
Bag it is
A mystery
For all I
Know!

Stuart Cranston (9)
Killyleagh Primary School

HIDDEN TREASURE

Hidden treasure on the beach
Where the palm trees twitch and wave
Upon the golden sand-like sun
Where I eat my coconut icy bun.

I am in the Caribbean
Drinking my tropic juice
I go in for a swim
It's a sparkly blue
They eat bananas too.

I get out the sea
With happiness full of glee
I sit on the sand
This is tropical land.

Robert Ferguson (10)
Killyleagh Primary School

NIGHT HUNT

Owls
Claws grabbing
Suddenly swooping
Like a white ghost in the bright moonlight
Soaring down like an arrow
A sudden squeak
Then silence
The kill
Made!

Timothy Morrison (8)
Killyleagh Primary School

IN THE SEA

Sunken ships deep down
Fish swimming all around

Pink and purple octopus
Tangling up on the ground

Sharks swimming side to side
And the treasure deep, deep down.

Amy Collins (8)
Killyleagh Primary School

HIDDEN TREASURES TO ME

Under the sea
What can there be?
Under the sea for me
There are cockles and mussels
Pebbles and fish
All these for me
Dolphins drift by
And whales cry
Mermaids with their golden hair
Capture pirate ships
While I eat my chips in yesterday's newspaper.
The tide is coming in
The sun is going down
The seagulls are getting weary
I love the sound of the sea
While the dugongs spread tears
Especially when the kestrels
Are out to get their meal
The sea is a world of treasures to me.

Tara Starbuck (9)
Killyleagh Primary School

SEASHORE

Pearly seashells sparkle bright,
Seas get rougher by the night,
Put a seashell to your ear,
Listen to the sound so quiet.

Pearls inside their rounded cases,
Waiting to be found by divers,
Washed upon the sunny beach,
Gleaming in the sun.

Golden fishes swim in shoals,
Silver eels do flips and tosses,
Slimy seaweed floating about,
The beach - a wonderful place.

Daryl Young (10)
Killyleagh Primary School

DEEP BLUE SEA

Down in the ocean
Deep below the waves
Creatures lurk in the dark domains
Octopuses, whales and giant squids
Is not all that lurks
In the dark domains.

Deeper to the bottom
Goblin sharks here and there
Look out over there, an angler fish's lair
And over there some tripods
Sea spiders race around
We must be nearing 5,000 feet
But there's more towards the ground.

Deeper into the sea trenches
Bricks lying on the ground
Could this be the way to Atlantis
It's finally been found
Over there Atlantis
An amazing sight to see
In this massive
Deep blue sea.

Johnathon Scott (10)
Killyleagh Primary School

UNDER MY BED!

Under my bed there's a cave
Where monsters live strong and brave
Sometimes I'm scared and weary
Hearing their voices so eerie
I cry in my bed
And my face it goes red
The monsters are out to get me!

Under my bed there are creatures
With big ferocious features
The moon is shining bright
It's the only source of light
I need to get their treasure
Before they get me!

There's something slimy on my leg
Oh don't hurt me I beg
Take my teddy,
Yes, little Freddy
But don't take me.

Rachelle Ross (9)
Killyleagh Primary School

UNDER THE BIG BLUE SEA

Under the big blue sea
The treasure has not been seen
All the fish play in a golden dish
There is a diver - that is me looking for the treasure
Crowns and jewels for the king
Rubies and sapphires for the queen
The secret has been revealed.

Steven Shields (8)
Killyleagh Primary School

THE TREASURE IN THE SEA

There's treasure in the sea
It is all for me
I'm going, going down
Into a new town
In a little sub.
It's all blue down here
In this thing I've hurt my ear.

My sub is black, blue and white
The seat belts in it are very tight
The seats are green and red
And it's lovely and warm.

There's bubbles floating everywhere
Oh look, oh look the treasure's there
Get it, get it, get it now
It's on the ship at the bow
Caught it, caught it, ahhh
There's an octopus after me.
Quickly, quickly get to sub
Oh I'm hungry, oh there's a biscuit
Yum, yum, yum.

Scott Rodgers (10)
Killyleagh Primary School

UNDER THE DEEP BLUE SEA

Under the deep blue sea
The treasure chest may be
Find the key and unlock the lock
There are treasures there for you and me.

Christopher Graham (9)
Killyleagh Primary School

MY POCKETS

There're lots of things in my pockets
Things you want to know
There're pens, pencils all sorts of things
Little treasures galore.

There're conkers brown and shiny
There's string that's whirly curly
There are things that fall out
There're things that go in
They are stuffed all together
My pockets of treasure.

Phillip Ferguson (10)
Killyleagh Primary School

THE SUN COMES OUT, YIPPEE!

I can see a squirrel picking up some nuts
Rabbits jumping everywhere having so much fun.

The sun comes out, yippee!
I play with my brother riding bikes all day
Drinking Coke, having such good fun.

The sun comes out, yippee!
Our family plays cricket outside
My dad hitting and I catching it
In a fast sort of way.

The sun goes down, oh no!
We go inside and get ready for bed
And I hate the end of the day.

Ryan Peden (9)
Milltown Primary School

UNDERWATER

If I was under the water
I would hunt for treasures
I would look and look
And I would not give up
Until I found it.

I would hire a submarine
That could dive a hundred metres
The treasures would be mine
I would jump until I burst into flames.

If I was under the sea
I would bounce on rocks
And it would be fun.

Victoria Baird (7)
Milltown Primary School

SPACE

If I could travel into space
That adventure would be ace
I'd travel in a purple bubble
That destroys any trouble.

If I could travel into space
I'd meet an alien with a green face
I'd travel and see all the planets
And meet aliens called Walanets!

If I could travel into space
I'd find a tree made of yellow lace
The animals there would really be scary
Some with short hair, some very hairy
I would be the *only* one who knew they were there.

Amelia White (10)
Milltown Primary School

SPRINGTIME

Springtime is here again
The farmer is so anxious
As the lambs and calves are born
Oh how I love to see
The lovely little white lambs and cute calves
As they try to stand up
One leg, two legs and a plop!
Down he falls but he tries again
And yes, he's on his feet.
I love spring.

Spring is when the air gets warmer
We don't have to stay inside all day
I love to climb the trees as my friends chase me.
The fields of clover are flattened as we roll on it
When we come back I smell of flowers.

Mark Peden (11)
Milltown Primary School

UNICORN

The white unicorn,
Has a big horn,
Above his nose,
But he has no foes,
He hibernates during the snow.

He drinks from the River Bann,
He eats aluminium from Coca-Cola cans,
He sleeps in a golden fire,
His popularity grows higher,
He lives where there is no barbed wire.

Matthew McAdam (11)
Milltown Primary School

BIRTHDAY

My birthday is coming
Think of all the things we can do
We can play all different sorts of games
Think of what we can do
Games are fun for parties
But just not any sort of party
A special party made especially for you.

Party time is over
We'll just have to wait
Another year
But sure you don't want to
Wait another year
Till the fun starts again.

Time is going slow
Wish it could be your birthday every day
But you can't have it every day
There'd be no room left.

Your mum will be going nuts
When she sees the mess you've made
All the presents everywhere
You could not move an inch
That's why I wouldn't want a birthday
Every day.

Sarah Hazlett (8)
Milltown Primary School

ONE MILLIMETRE TALL

If you were only one millimetre tall
You'd ride a snail to school.
If you were only one millimetre tall
A crumb of chocolate cake would be a big feast
It would last seven days.

If you were only one millimetre tall
Your bed would be made of a matchbox and wool.
If you were only one millimetre tall
A fly would be a beast to you
If you were only one millimetre tall
It would take a year to carry a pencil to your room
If you were only one millimetre tall
You would have to hug your mum's little finger.

If you were only one millimetre tall
You would understand this poem
This poem took me eighteen years
Because I am one millimetre tall.

Jenny Peden (8)
Milltown Primary School

THE PHOENIX

These fiery red-hot birds
Have golden, shiny wings
And red ruby eyes.

These birds live for five hundred years
They are friends to the deer
And other animals in the forest.

When they die they burn themselves
Then a younger bird
Rises from the black ashes.

These wonderful birds
Are sadly myths and legends.
Do you want to know their name?

The phoenix.

Carrie Lennon (11)
Milltown Primary School

MY BIRTHDAY

My birthday is my favourite day
And I go out to play
My friends would say
Come and play.

I'll bounce and bounce all day
My birthday is my favourite day

My birthday is my favourite day
I'll eat cake
I invited Jake
My birthday is my favourite day.

My birthday is my favourite day
But it's over and I have to go to bed
My birthday is my favourite day.

Sarah McAdam (8)
Milltown Primary School

IT'S ALL FOR ME

In the deep, blue sea
I saw a fishy
It led me into a dark, drippy cave
I saw this little glow
And then it started to show
There were fish all around me
All kinds of colours
While I was admiring all the fish then *crash!*
There it was in front of me - the chest
It was so bright I nearly got blinded
It was a glare
It could even blind our Prime Minister,
Tony Blair.
There was gold, jewellery, but no sweets
But who cares I'll just bring this home
And that will be my adventure
And I did it all alone
I have found the treasure
In the deep, blue sea
And the best thing about it,
It's all for *me!*

Holly Lockhart (9)
Poyntzpass Primary School

I MIGHT BE A TREASURE

Maybe I am a treasure
Everyone calls me that
Maybe I have something.
I could be rich
I could be famous
Wait, I'm not rich or famous
But why?

I could have a lot of money in my bank account
No I do not have that much.
Maybe they like me
They always give me sweets
They give me great things
It's just because they like me!

John Irvine (11)
Poyntzpass Primary School

FAMILY TREASURE

Hidden treasure everywhere,
I think I'll find some over there
In the canal far away,
I think I'll find it, maybe today.

I think I see a treasure box,
Or maybe it's just dirty rocks
I hope it's not a fish's nest,
Oh I really want that treasure chest.

So then I opened it happily
And saw pictures of my family
I stopped and looked at the photos blurred,
Then it hit me how much I really cared.

So now today I'll just say,
I have my treasure anyway
I don't need silver or any gold,
As long as I have my family to hold!

Hannah Liggett (11)
Poyntzpass Primary School

I Found Grandma

I was in a submarine
With nothing to be seen
Down, down and down
Past tunnels and fish
Then I heard a woman say
'Get three wishes on the way.'
That was strange, who's on board
Down in the submarine?
Then I found her,
It was Grandma!
'Wake up!
Wake up!
Mum! Mum! I was in a submarine.'
'No, you weren't! You just had a bad dream.'

Rebekah Denny (8)
Poyntzpass Primary School

Hidden Treasures

I was sailing on a boat to Jamaica
Suddenly the boat stopped
A tornado was approaching
The boat was going to sink.
'Shut up all those portholes
We don't want to die,' said one of the passengers.
Do not panic.
We are sinking, look at those jewels
                    in a treasure box!

Mark Cairns (7)
Poyntzpass Primary School

MY GRANDAD

The hidden treasures in the sand
My mum needs to go to the band.
My dad and I have to go to the sea and go diving.
I will dig in the sand for the treasure.
At the beach Dad went diving.
I dug in the sand
Then Dad and I lay down
I heard people talking.
I opened one eye and saw two men with the treasure,
I saw where they put it, so I got it.
I saw my grandad in a picture.
I would not like to lose it.

Kyle Walker (7)
Poyntzpass Primary School

OCTOPUS

In the sea
An octopus swam,
Round and round and round
With his legs
One, two, three.
Round and round
Four, five six,
Very quickly,
    seven,
        eight!

Louise Robinson (8)
Poyntzpass Primary School

MY TREASURE

I have a treasure,
It is pink and white,
It is my teddy,
Her eyes sparkle in the light.

I have a treasure,
She is special to me,
I got her when I was born,
Sometimes Emma, my sister, gets her
                       and puts her on the settee.

I have a treasure,
I keep it in my bed,
I wouldn't change her,
For money instead.

Amy Liggett (8)
Poyntzpass Primary School

MAN UNITED

M an United's in the lead.
A ndy Cole is in the team.
N eil is scoring a goal.

U seless Arsenal is way behind.
N eil is doing a header now.
I am a goalie and I save a goal
T wo people are in defence.
E d is the coach
D ad's team is no good

Alan Wilson (8)
Poyntzpass Primary School

MEMORIES OF FAMILY AND FRIENDS

Treasure in a chest is second best
It's memories that count,
Memories of fun times,
Memories of friends,
Memories of people who drive you round the bend.

Family are also very important
My mum, my dad, my brother
All the rest of my family
Crazy auntie Hilly and all my cousins
They are all treasures to me.

My conclusion of this poem is
Money doesn't matter
It is memories and family that count.

James Rooney (11)
Poyntzpass Primary School

UNDER THE SEA

Under the sea we go, go, go,
Discovering the secrets of the deep blue sea.
Watching the octopus go to the bottom of the sea.
The birds are chirping at the top of the water,
Saying, 'Hope you have fun.'
I went to the top and shouted
'That was fun but I'm too cold in the water.'
It is fun to explore the ocean.
It is exciting too.
So many discoveries too!

Stephanie Henry (8)
Poyntzpass Primary School

HIDDEN TREASURES

Down below the deep blue sea
The treasure is hidden,
But only the pirates know.
The ship has sank
So the treasures are under the sea
One day I was sailing on my ship
Then I spotted the treasures in the sea
I brought it home.

Neil Anderson (8)
Poyntzpass Primary School

BETTY SPAGHETTI

I have two dolls called Zoe and Betty
I play with them a lot.
I change their clothes around:
Sometimes I change their arms and legs.
Then, when I have finished playing with them
I put them away in the bag for the night.

Rachel Bryson (8)
Poyntzpass Primary School

THE WISH

I wish I was a monkey,
I wish, I wish, I wish.
I wish I was a grown-up,
I wish, I wish, I wish.
All the things that I wished, I wish they would come true.

Cathy Wilson (8)
Poyntzpass Primary School

HIDDEN TREASURES

My family have been lost from me,
For oh, so many years,
To find them would be a great joy
And bring so many tears.

I have found my family,
So now I have four sparkling treasures,
My mum, dad, sister and brother,
They are special to me in all different measures.

My four sparkling treasures are extraordinary
In many different ways,
But they are precious and valuable,
For oh, so many days.

I am so fortunate to have them,
If I put them together,
They would be like a pot of gold
Shining fantastically, with light forever.

I will never let them go again,
I will be helpful, cheerful and gentle
And I hope they will be faithful, generous and loyal to me,
I love my family but sometimes, my brother and sister
Are mental.

Leanne Walker (10)
Poyntzpass Primary School

MY FAMILY TREASURE

I found the treasure
A year ago
When I was cleaning my granny's room
I found the photo in an old cupboard drawer
There he stood, tall and proud
In a black and white photograph
It was my great granda.

The dust had covered it over
When my granny saw the photo
It brought a tear to her eye
She began to tell a story
About long, long ago
When he went to the war
Granny took a photo that remains with her today.

This old photo to you might not
Seem valuable but it's valuable to us
With his uniform on he looked so smart
As he went to fight for our country
In the Second World War.
My family treasure is not gold
It's a photo of my great granda
In his uniform.

Samantha Hazlett (11)
Poyntzpass Primary School

HIDDEN TREASURES

I am a boy called Tyrone Linden,
I have a pet parrot called Sammy.
I was sitting in front of the TV,
I was watching a film called
Hidden Treasure.

It was a fantastic film,
It was about a sailor with a parrot,
Looking for a treasure chest.
They looked and looked for days
But they could not find it.

The second episode of the film
Will be next week.
That film gave me a thought,
So the next day I got up very early,
I went into a garage and built
A machine for going under the ocean.

So I phoned my uncle to give me a hand
And told him all that I was going to do.
I am going to look for hidden treasure
Under the Irish Sea.
I will bring my auntie, uncle,
Mummy, Daddy, my sister
And my four cousins.

Tyrone Linden (9)
Poyntzpass Primary School

HIDDEN TREASURES

One day I was playing football
Toe-tapping and shooting
But I struck it hard over the wall
I clambered up the wall and saw a chest

I opened the chest
And I saw stairs leading round and down into pitch-black
I tramped down them
Trying not to slack

I slowly walked down, *bang!*
Every stair glowed luminous green
It was getting very exciting
One of the strangest places I've ever seen

Then the stairs went up
And before I knew it I was on a football pitch
Old Trafford a sign read
That looked exceedingly rich

I walked into the stand and watched them play
It was the Manchester United team training
They called me on and gave me their autograph
And they gave me a ball for playing when it was raining

This is my treasure
A treasure for me
You may think this is stupid
But it's a ball full of glee.

Sam Lockhart (10)
Poyntzpass Primary School

THE LOST STONE

Himalayas here I come
I reached the top above the clouds
My instructor told me on the ground
'Don't stop never give up'
But I said to myself, 'You stupid old pain
You don't know the first thing about climbing.'
But the next thing I knew I had fallen down a crack.

I woke up.
Old men were around me.
They said, 'Will you help us find the stone,
Our village is wrecked without it.'

I got out of the cave and I looked for about a week
Or two.
I was so tired that I fell down another crack.

I walked out patiently.
I stood on a stone and fell down into the ground.
I saw the lost stone.
Queer wee men came out
And I threw them down a cliff
And snatched the stone.

I returned it to the village.
The people gave me a dinner
But when I touched the roast beef
The teacher shouted at me.
It turned out in the end I was daydreaming.

Josh Ferris (10)
Poyntzpass Primary School

IS IT SILVER AND GOLD?

One day my mum said
That she had some treasure
The treasure was for me
I thought it might be
Sparkling silver and gold.

I asked my mum if it was
Silver and gold
She said it isn't
Silver and gold
It is a family award.

My mum said
It's about one hundred years old
It was given to me
By my mother and to her
By my grandmother.

Our family think it's so special
I was given it when
I was nine years old
And it shall go
On through all the generations.

The family award was
A medal for the best sports-person
At netball and hockey
In the school.

So now you know
That's what our treasure was.

Naomi Clarke (9)
Poyntzpass Primary School

THE MOST IMPORTANT TREASURE

In the morning before you're awake
I'll be under Acton Lake
Trying to find a chest of treasure
So I can have a life of pleasure.

I was up at the crack of dawn
Which was very early in the morn
Looking to find this precious chest
And where it might have stopped to rest.

I thought I saw something over there
Or maybe it was just a dirty blur
But then I saw a chest so clean
And it was the best I'd ever seen.

I quickly opened it with care
And found that there were
Old photos of my relatives
These are much better than what treasure gives.

Look, there's Auntie Mabel
Under the huge, brown table
And agile Uncle Tim
At the local gym.

Look, there's Aunt Anne
Burning the expensive pan
And humorous Uncle Mike
Riding his sporty bike.

You can have a life of pleasure
Without any golden treasure
And have friends and family too
For caring when you've got things like the flu.

Sandra Meredith (10)
Poyntzpass Primary School

I WOULD BE . . .

As an animal I would be a fox,
cunning and quick.

As a colour I would be red,
warm and clean.

As a bird, I would be a robin,
small and quiet.

As a flower I would be a daffodil,
comforting and stylish.

As a character I would be James Bond,
sophisticated and up-to-date.

As a musical instrument, I would be the drums,
cool and powerful.

Andy Boal (11)
Redburn Primary School

I WOULD BE . . .

As an animal I would be a Lion,
Proud, fierce and fast-running.
As a colour I would be Yellow,
Rejuvenating, happy and very playful.
As a flower I would be a Venus flytrap,
Instinctive, monstrous and well adapted.
As a character, I would be Angelica,
Bossy greedy and very, very pretty.
As a musical instrument I would be Chimes,
Cheerful and very, very noisy.

Sarah-Jane Carruthers (10)
Redburn Primary School

I Would Be

As an animal I would be a puppy,
Kind, loving, young and very inquisitive.

As a colour, I would be red,
Forgiving, loving, warm, bright-red rose.

As a bird I would be a robin,
Soft, friendly, sneaky, quiet and
Most of all happy.

As a flower I would be a rose,
Kind, loving, stylish and perfect,
(A bright-red rose)

As an instrument I would be a keyboard,
Quiet, relaxing, peaceful, soothing and joyful.

As a character I would be Winnie the Pooh,
Fun, loving, playful and quite adventurous.

Zoe McDevitt (11)
Redburn Primary School

Wind

I listen until I hear the crazy, whirling, hurling
sound smashing almost everywhere.

It rages like a furious bull.
It's frightening.

The monster screams, shouts and collides with vehicles,
then looks for another target.

I stay indoors, safe and sound from the monster wind.

Luke McCall (11)
Redburn Primary School

SNAKE

He slides and slithers through the grass
And coils himself around a tree
His forked tongue shooting in and out
As he hisses at the frightened visitors.

His camouflaged scaly skin helping him
Hide among the trees
Winding his long, thin body
Waiting to bite with his sharp teeth.

He thinks of the rainforest
Paradise to him
Free to do what he wants
Hunting for his own prey
Wriggling and playing with his mate
But instead he lives his life
Locked in a concrete cage.

Gemma Kilby (10)
Redburn Primary School

HYENA

He stares at the people walking by
Licking his black-grey fur
While staring at the people he wishes he could reach
His claws scraping against the wall.
He is in rapid rage.
He tries to get out but he fails.
He should be in his cave in the jungle
Sniggering at other animals
Howling under trees
Hunting for his prey
But instead he howls angrily at the bright moon.

Stewart Mitchell (10)
Redburn Primary School

LEOPARD

The leopard whines in the corner, wanting to be free.
Children bang on his glass cage
He crouches in long grass wanting a deer
But he gets his food thrown in to him.

His spotted skin makes him look so graceful
He tries to hide from visitors
He wishes he could be having fun, playing with his cubs
Tries to break up the rolling ball of fighting cubs.

He should be in the jungle
His sharp eyes catching the sprinting of a zebra
Making sure his family are protected from danger
But instead he growls at visitors.

Peter Murray (10)
Redburn Primary School

INSIDE OUTSIDE

Outside.

Cold, wind.

Play, shiver, struggle.

Birds washing . . . fire, beds.

Sleep, snuggle, warm-up.

Warm, cosy.

Inside.

Hannah-Rose Henning (10)
Redburn Primary School

OSTRICH

He walks with long, slim legs
People stare at his beautiful black and white feathers
Wishes for freedom.
He shows off his feathers, stamping his feet because he is angry.

He thinks he should be near lakes
Walking proudly around, holding his head up high.

Tiptoes on his delicate pink feet
Fluffs out his black and white feathers
His long neck reaches up to the sky.

He wishes he could see his young
And sprint through the long grass.

If only he could kick his way out of this terrible cage.

Sam Yates (9)
Redburn Primary School

BROTHER AND SISTER

Brother

Sensible   cool

Annoy   punch   fight

Muck   football   dress   dolls

Moan   beg   skip

Clean   beautiful

Sister.

Scott Rankin (10)
Redburn Primary School

ONE WET AND WINDY DAY

The wind growls like a lion
Lifts tiles off roofs
Makes trees tap against windows
And blows you down the street.

The rain floods the grass
Bounces on the ground
And drenches your socks.

On a stormy day the sky is dull and grey
The clouds are thick and heavy
It makes you want to cry.

I would rather sit in front of a fire
And drink hot cocoa.

Jonathan Jackson (9)
Redburn Primary School

INSIDE OUTSIDE

Inside

Boring   stuffy

Sit   read   sleep

Walls   doors   birds   grass

Play   skip   jog

Breezy   fresh

Outside

Rachel Pardon (10)
Redburn Primary School

MY KITTEN

My kitten is fluffy
His fur is black and white
His eyes are brown
With a greeny light
He is so playful
He paws the wool all day
Sometimes he even runs away.

Niall Dornan (8)
St Colman's Abbey Primary School, Newry

MY CHUM, LASSIE

L   assie is my really best chum,
A   lways loving to run in the glorious summer sun.
S   he barks at the rabbits from her pen at night,
S   he's a kindly dog when children are in sight.
I   really wish that she could talk,
E   ven to ask me to go for a walk.

Férgal McEvoy (9)
St Colman's Abbey Primary School, Newry

EGG THOUGHTS

Boiled egg.
I don't like your inside.
I don't like the way you slide.
When you fall I shiver as you splatter like a wild river.
I could go for many days without a soft-boiled egg.

Damien Lamph (9)
St Colman's Abbey Primary School, Newry

WINTER COMES

Winter comes
With frost, fog and ice.

Winter comes
With spiky icicles.

Winter comes
With snow covered streets.

Winter comes
With Jack Frost biting at my fingers, toes and nose.

Winter comes
With wind, rain, snow and gales blowing.

Keelan Cunningham (9)
St Colman's Abbey Primary School, Newry

SPRING

Spring comes
with branches budding.
Spring comes
with green splashes.
Spring comes
with no long nights.
Spring comes
with beautiful blue skies.
Spring comes
my favourite time.

Eamonn Noade (9)
St Colman's Abbey Primary School, Newry

SPOOKS COME

Spooks come and
Spook me out.
Spooks come and
Witches no doubt.
Spooks come more
And more every time.
Spooks come sometimes
They spook me out of my mind.
Spooks come
Naughty and kind.
Spooks come looking
For a child.
Spooks come looking for me,
But it's a good job I can't be seen.

Konor Smith (8)
St Colman's Abbey Primary School, Newry

THE MONSTER

Fingers bony and thin
Sliding over my dad's
His head's large and his body huge.
He turned and I saw his face
With green warts, sharp yellow teeth
And a nose, green and pointy
His blood-shot eyes
Stared at me
I screamed and shouted
'Monster!'

Matthew Crimmins (9)
St Colman's Abbey Primary School, Newry

NEVER LOOK UNDER THE BED

Never look under the bed
for that is where the bogeyman's found
where rats and cats lie.
Never look under the bed
for that is where the green goblins lurk
in the darkest corners.
Never look under the bed
your bones and flesh might be
torn to shreds.
Never look under the bed
for ghosts camouflage themselves
ready to pounce.
Then you're dead.

James Dickson (9)
St Colman's Abbey Primary School, Newry

WINTERTIME

Winter comes with ice and snow
Winter comes with snowmen too
Winter comes with people throwing snowballs
Winter comes with watery slush
Winter comes with sparkling snowflakes
Winter comes with freezing icicles
Winter comes with hats, gloves, coats and scarves
Winter comes with hot coal fires
Winter comes with the hungry robin.

Daniel O'Hare (8)
St Colman's Abbey Primary School, Newry

ALL ABOUT SCHOOL

Children running
and screaming
in the playground.

Hands and arms
getting cut on all the
sharp bricks on the school wall.

Children running
playing yo-yo
or tag.

When time is up
a boy comes out
with a handbell,
shaking it.
Clang! Clang! Clang!

Children going upstairs
and teachers asking
them questions till 3 o'clock.

Glenn O'Neill (9)
St Colman's Abbey Primary School, Newry

SPRING

S   pring has arrived
P   leasant weather fills the sky
R   ows of daffodils begin to emerge
I   cicles are no longer to be seen
N   ewborn lambs skip around the soft green grass
G   ardens now begin to spring to life.

Kelvin McKenna (9)
St Colman's Abbey Primary School, Newry

THE VAMPIRE WHO LOST HIS FANGS

The vampire who lost his fangs
Didn't know where to find them.
He looked up, he looked down,
He looked near, and all around.
Oh where, oh where are the vampire's fangs.

The vampire who lost his fangs
Looked in his cupboard,
Looked in his bed,
But all he found there was a victim's head.
Where, oh where are the vampire's fangs.

He lay on the couch screaming and crying,
Just wanting to find his fangs.
Then out of the blue he got a strange parcel,
And inside the parcel were his fangs,
His long, curved bloodsucking fangs
So watch out, he is back for you.

Declan Black (9)
St Colman's Abbey Primary School, Newry

WINTER

Winter is coming, old people get warm.
My mum is unhappy in winter
But my friends and I like winter.
One night it snowed.
The next day we were snowed in.
We looked for a way out.
We got no food to eat all day,
So we dug our way out.

Cathal Harte (8)
St Colman's Abbey Primary School, Newry

I HAD A

I had a bug
Who played in a rug.

I had a cat
Who ate a delectable rat.

I had a daisy
But I was really too lazy
To water it.

I had a ghost
Who liked to eat some toast.

I had a goblin
With the strange name, Bobblin.

I had a dog
Who slept like a log.

Caolan Travers (9)
St Colman's Abbey Primary School, Newry

FOOD

I took a dish and it was delicious.
Yummy, yummy in my tummy.
This pasta and rice - it tastes so nice
And looks so neat, it's too good to eat.
I love custard and jelly that fills up my belly.
All this food is so good,
But please tell me this dish will not be a fish.
I give a huge sigh when I start on the pie,
But my mum's bolognese sends me into a daze.

Anton McLaughlin (9)
St Colman's Abbey Primary School, Newry

SPRING

Along the country roads, meadows.
In the meadows, burrows.
In the burrows, rabbits.

In the meadows, calves
Skipping like children,
While cows crunch grass.

Hares bounce left and right.
I'd love to live with them,
Feed with them,
Play with them.

Caolan Moan (8)
St Colman's Abbey Primary School, Newry

CREATURES

A whale, so big, a fish, so small.
In the jungle, a lion so fierce
Going to get its prey
Before the day is gone.
A slippery snake high on a branch
Not moving, just sleeping.
A cheetah, so fast
It could catch a giraffe.
Eagles so high in their cliff-top nests
Guarding their eggs.

Sean Kane (8)
St Colman's Abbey Primary School, Newry

SERPENTS

Slimy serpents slither around me while snapping at my heels,
My heart is throbbing while I stare straight into the eyes of their
                              high and mighty king of snakes,
While my eyes are transfixed on him as he is hypnotically seducing me.
When I awake I find myself alone in a temple, lost in the mists of time.

Ronan Mallon (9)
St Colman's Abbey Primary School, Newry

HAPPINESS

Happiness is bright blue
like a nice sunny,
summer's sky.

It is the taste
of a ripe melon,
melting in your mouth.

It is the smell
of tropical flowers,
shining on an island.

It is the look
of a calm sea,
floating in the mild breeze.

It is the sweet
sound of the nightingale
on a still evening.

It is the feeling of cosiness
sitting beside an open log fire
on a stormy, winter's night.

Declan McNally (11)
St Colman's Primary School, Newry

PLAYGROUND

The playground is noisy and full of joy and laughter
People shouting, people playing,
People dancing, falling, people racing,
People turning.

The playground is full of people
Playing football, running,
Playing racing and competitions.

The playground is a joyful place
As friends come together to play and chat.
The playground is a sad place,
Sometimes friends fight and shout.
The playground is a silent place
As friends return to class.

Richard McNally (11)
St Colman's Primary School, Newry

FRIENDS

F   unny friends are cheerful
R   eady to play all day
I   ncredibly exciting
E   nergetic in every way
N   ever leave you lonely
D   on't make you sad
S   pecial friends are there for you
     when you're feeling bad.

Richella Canavan (10)
St Colman's Primary School, Newry

AT THE FEIS

I sit on my seat
Waiting to be called.
'Number 41 please!'
Oh no, that's me.

I walk up very nervously
Then I stand behind the curtain
With two big red cheeks,
Here I go, wish me luck!

I stand on the yellow ticket
Nearly ready to start
She nods her head quickly
Oh no! What is the first line of my poem?
I try to think.

No, it is not coming to my head.
What will I do?
My hands are shaking.
My tummy's aching.
'Please start,' the judge shouts to me three times.
Ah, ah, yes I've remembered, it's at half-past three.

Riona Canavan (10)
St Colman's Primary School, Newry

THE MAN FROM SHINN

There was an old man from Shinn
Who loved to play the violin
He was playing all day
Then someone did say,
'Shut up or I'll put you in the bin.'

Nicola McEvoy (11)
St Colman's Primary School, Newry

DUSTBINS

I think instead of having one bin
We should have four.
Three for recycling and
One for things you
Don't want anymore.

Just think of the things
We waste every day.
Glass bottles, old tins, paper
They all go the wrong way.

Instead of having one bin
Four would be grand.
I wish that people
Would understand
That we only have one world
And we should protect our land.

Niamh McGowan (11)
St Colman's Primary School, Newry

FRIEND

F   aithful, kind and always true,
R   eassuring through and through,
I   nsightful in your wise advice,
E   nthusiastic, sweet and nice,
N   oted for your smiling face -
D   ear friend, no one could take your place.

Eamon Keenan (11)
St Colman's Primary School, Newry

TIME FOR A WALK

The sun has come up
The sky is blue
I look at my watch
Half-past two
I call out
Time for a walk
Tyson comes barking
As if he can talk
He comes into the kitchen
To get his lead
I tell him to sit
He takes no heed
We walk round Cooper's and back,
We need a long rest after that.

Sinead McGahan (11)
St Colman's Primary School, Newry

HANDS

Hands of people help us to our jobs,
Hands help teachers write and correct,
Hands of mechanics have to be strong and tough,
Hands of ladies are slim, gentle and slender,
Hands of children are minute and soft,
Hands can also cause discomfort or damage,
Hands can also be comforting and peacemaking.

Darragh Murphy (11)
St Colman's Primary School, Newry

HANDS

The hands of children
are tiny and gentle.
The hands of ladies
are soft and loving.
The hands of a granny
are wrinkled and warm.

The hands of a builder
are strong and rough.
The hands of a typist
are nimble and quick.
The hands of painters
are skilful and delicate.

Sarah Redmond (11)
St Colman's Primary School, Newry

A LETTER TO MR BECKHAM

Dear Mr Beckham,
Were you once like me?
Did you play football in the playground?
Did you wish for half-past three?
Did you dream of only football
And of lifting the FA Cup?
Did you believe you would play
For your country and that you
Would captain them?
Do you believe that dreams come true?
Because I think they do.

Aidan Digney (11)
St Colman's Primary School, Newry

THE DAY I WENT TO THE ZOO

There's plenty to see and a lot to do,
There's a Frigate bird and a tiny shrew;
There's a Vesper rat and a two-toed sloth,
And it's fair to say that I like them both.
There's a Canada goose and a polar bear
And things that come from everywhere.
There are lots of things that you've never seen
Like the kinkajou and the wolverine.
You really have to go to the zoo
To see a newborn wallaroo
Or a fallow deer or a white-tailed gnu.
There are wondrous birds on a beautiful lake,
There's a timber wolf and hognose snake.
There are animals with great appeal,
Like the hummingbird and the harbour seal.
There are pony rides, there are birds of prey,
And something happening every day.
There are wolves and foxes, hawks and owls,
And a great big pit where the lion prowls.
There are quiet pools and pleasant cages,
Where reptiles lie and the tiger rages.
The houses are clean, the keepers are kind,
And one baboon has a pink behind.
The entire aim of a well-kept zoo
Is to bring the animal kingdom to you.

Rachel Gardiner (10)
St James's Primary School, Hillsborough

THE ALIEN

I was looking through my telescope,
When suddenly I saw,
A small, green figure,
About three feet tall.

He had a purple nose,
And rabbit ears,
And four bright eyes,
With two feet and forty toes!

Claudia Kinloch (9)
St James's Primary School, Hillsborough

MY GARDEN

Down at the bottom of my garden,
In my hideout, my secret den,
It's hidden behind tall grass,
I creep down there to play each day.

I love the snails and rabbit trails,
I follow them through the grass,
We hide and creep,
Play hide and seek,
It's great fun I'd love to stay.

One day I was down in my den,
Playing with the rabbits and snails,
Then out of the blue,
A lion appeared, alive and true.

'Oh help,' I cried and screamed,
But he did not want to beam,
In his paw there was a thorn,
And the fur it had been torn,
He sat there weeping and sad.

I pulled it out,
He ran about,
And stayed in my secret den,
Down at the bottom of my garden.

Frances Thompson (10)
St James's Primary School, Hillsborough

THE THING AT THE BACK OF THE CLASSROOM

The boy at the back of the classroom
Convinces us all he's a child.
I don't even think he's human
But something weird and wild.

He never answers questions
Or puts up his hand,
I think he speaks another language
That we can't understand.

He must be really different
When he's out of his disguise,
He might have big antennae
And fifteen thousand eyes!

He could be from Uranus
Or maybe from the moon.
But to me he's just the weird boy
Who sits at the back of the room.

Poppy Harvey (10)
St James's Primary School, Hillsborough

SNOWFLAKES

Snowflakes tumbling down
like an acrobat rolling around.
Snowflakes swaying down
like a child on a swing.
Snowflakes going down, down, down,
then hit the ground to melt,
then start all over again.

Jack Thompson (8)
St James's Primary School, Hillsborough

A WEEK WITH DRAGON

Today I found a dragon,
Outside on the garden seat,
He's green and scaly and quite small,
And when he yawns I feel the heat.

Dragon burnt the sofa,
And almost Mum and Dad,
Mum is turning purple,
Dad is getting mad.

I've told him to be good
And though he knows he should,
There's no way he would.

Dragon's mum and dad came,
(They say his name is Max),
Now that he's away
My parents can relax.

I'm really missing Dragon
I wish he would come back
Now that he's away
A dragon's what I lack.

The house is clean again,
It's no longer a mess,
But now I'm feeling sad,
Because I'm dragonless.

Dragon's back again
Plus 27 more
They're driving Mum insane
And there's claw marks on the floor.

Rebecca Watson (10)
St James's Primary School, Hillsborough

SNOWFLAKES

Snowflakes fluttering down
Crashing to the ground
They are little athletes
Tumbling down
What will happen to them?
They glitter through the night
Snowflake bye, bye.

Neil Mulholland (7)
St James's Primary School, Hillsborough

SNOWFLAKES

Spinning round like the world
away from the clouds.
Going down, down and down
floating down from the sky
to hit the ground.
Splat, splat, splat.

Neil McDonald (8)
St James's Primary School, Hillsborough

SNOWFLAKES

Snowflakes, snowflakes on the ground
Swirling, swirling right around
When they all touch the ground
Sparkling, sparkling on the ground
It just reminds me of the crow in the snow
Turned into the glittery crow.

Adam Patterson (8)
St James's Primary School, Hillsborough

DREAMS

Dreams of fairies,
Dreams of trees,
Dreams that have
Beautiful things.

Some are scary,
Some are nice,
Ones of princesses,
Ones of mice.

But of course,
They'll never come true
I hope I won't
Tell mine to you!

Judith Crow (10)
St James's Primary School, Hillsborough

SNOWFLAKES

I saw a little snowflake on the 23rd December
It was fluttering down and looked lovely falling down
I was playing outside while they were fluttering down
Then they hit the ground
They went on every kind of road
Snowflakes are all different sizes
That we see.

These little snowflakes are lovely to see
I like to see snowflakes at wintertime.

Hannah Wilson (7)
St James's Primary School, Hillsborough

SNOWFLAKES

Snowflakes tumbling down
Just like little acrobats.
They look just lovely don't they?
But then when they hit the ground
Splash!
Goodbye, goodbye, goodbye!

Lucy La Marche (8)
St James's Primary School, Hillsborough

SNOWFLAKES

Falling right down,
Falling on the ground.
Pitter, patter, pitter, patter,
Falling all around,
Sometimes they make me frown.

David Houston (8)
St James's Primary School, Hillsborough

SNOWFLAKES

Snowflakes, snowflakes fluttering down
Like a butterfly in its dressing gown
They fall on the ground and have a big splat
Winter is gone but it will come back
And I know it will because it's the top season.

Natasha Wilson (8)
St James's Primary School, Hillsborough

MY BIRTHDAY

Hip-hip
It's my birthday
I am 10 today
I will get presents and cards
My friends will come to play
Hip-hip
It's my birthday
Today.

Christopher McCauley (10)
St James's Primary School, Hillsborough

SNOWFLAKES

Snowflakes are coming down, now hide
They're coming down like little butterflies
They look a bit prickly and a bit dangly
Look, they're very glittery
Oh look at the lake it has turned to ice
Now they're away
Now can I go?

Rebecca Rankin (8)
St James's Primary School, Hillsborough

SNOWFLAKES

Snowflakes tumbling down
Practising their acrobatics
Falling down from the sky
Spreading all around the earth
Children playing in the snow
Having fun in the snow.

James Standard (7)
St James's Primary School, Hillsborough

My Surprise

I awoke at 5.30am
I was very excited, it was Christmas morning.
I sneaked downstairs, frightened in case he was still there.
I went to my mum and dad and said, 'Please get up, please get up.'
We all walked slowly towards the living room.
I opened the door,
I turned on the light.
There it was shining,
Orange, black and white.
It looked so big, would I be able to get on it?
I could not believe it.
My KTM 65cc scrambler,
What a Christmas!

Thomas Beck (10)
St James's Primary School, Hillsborough

My School

My school is so cool,
The teachers rule,
You'll get loads of friends,
When you come to my school.

School starts at nine,
And ends just in time,
We do PE and history,
And dance and science,
That's what you do when you come to my school.

Sarah Quinn (10)
St James's Primary School, Hillsborough

MRS HOBBLE

Mrs Hobble our school teacher,
Is the worst teacher anybody could ever have,
She's got warts on her nose,
She's got evil, blue eyes and she crunches her
Apples when we work, how distracting!

Mrs Hobble is very cheeky,
She's also very sneaky,
She's forty-five,
And I'm sorry she survived
That horrible hurricane!

That's the story of Mrs Hobble,
The one that gets us into trouble!

Ciera Beck (10)
St James's Primary School, Hillsborough

MY DOG

My dog is called Charlie,
Her fur is coloured golden,
She would give anything to go for a walk.

Last year my nanny and pappy bought her a bone for Christmas,
I got her a toy and a bowl for her birthday when she was two,
One day I was out for a walk, when she dug up a hole and lifted
out a bone.

On a cold night we would bring her inside and she would lie in
front of the fire,
The cat loves to lie on her back when they are sleeping.

Andrew La Marche (10)
St James's Primary School, Hillsborough

MY CARAVAN

I have a caravan in Benone
I never go there all alone
My family of five go there for fun
It is really, really great, you should come!

There is an outdoor swimming pool
The water can sometimes be quite cool
I swim in it
To make me fit
It is really, really great, you should come!

I go to the park
To have a lark
I play on the swing
On it I love to sing
It is really, really great, you should come!

The beach is not too far away
When you go there you don't have to pay
We swim in the sea and have lots of fun
When we get out we need something in our tum
Then we would catch crabs and fish
We think they make quite a tasty dish
It is really, really great, you should come!
I love the caravan.

Nicola Carlisle (9)
St James's Primary School, Hillsborough

FAT CAT

Big cat, small cat, fat and thin
Long cat, short cat, out and in.
Hot cat, cool cat, brown and white
Spotty cat, stripy cat, that's all right!

Wall cat, ground cat, patched and plain
Painted cat, wild cat, look at that mane.
Smart cat, dumb cat, wet and dry
Cheeky cat, kind cat, cats are *sly!*

Hannah McCarthy (10)
St James's Primary School, Hillsborough

CHRISTMAS DAY

Christmas Day was a great surprise,
Nanny came round and said, 'Close your eyes,'
Mum led the way to the garden shed,
'Nan, where are you taking us,' my brother said.
Mum stood back as Nan took us in,
'Shhh, children, don't make a din.'

'Open your arms put out your hands
A soft ball of fluff is about to land.'
We opened our eyes and couldn't believe,
What wonderful presents we had just received,
Two little bunnies looked up at me,
I felt so happy and full of glee.

'Oh nanny I love you,' my brother exclaimed,
'I can't wait to tell my cousin, Jane.'
'What will you call them?' my nanny asked!
'I'll call mine . . . Benji,' said my brother at last.
'What about you?' said Steven to me,
'Oh I think I'll call mine . . . Little Flopsie.'

Suzanna Walker (10)
St John's Primary School, Hillsborough

MY WEEK

Monday swimming, table tennis
I do that day,
Tuesday BB I do like to go,
Wednesday football, my favourite sport.
Thursday art, my best picture to do,
Friday the last day of school,
Saturday hip, hip hooray, school off today,
Sunday church to sing to our royal King.

Matthew McClune (9)
St John's Primary School, Hillsborough

HARRY

Harry thinks he is so cool with his blond flick,
Yet it makes me sick,
He thinks he is popular with all the girls,
Harry thinks he is so strong yet he really does pong,
He thinks he is a teacher's pet but I know who is,
He thinks he is a whizz on a computer but I'm much better.

Richard Cousins (9)
St John's Primary School, Hillsborough

ROBOTS

If I had a robot . . .
That would be so great.
I could bring it into school
And the kids would say
'Wow . . . that's cool!'

I would take him out to play . . .
He'd win catch every day.
With a flip and a flop
Off he would go . . .
All the grass he could mow!

Mark Thompson (8)
St John's Primary School, Hillsborough

DOGS

Dogs are interesting
Dogs are fun
They like to run about in the sun.
They are soft to touch.
We like them very much
They are a good little bunch
And always eat their lunch
They play together for now and forever.

Joanna Guthrie (8)
St John's Primary School, Hillsborough

I LOVE ANIMALS

I have a cat, dog, hamster and fish
My dog is funny because when I take him for a walk
He keeps biting his leash.

My cat eats so much food it's getting too fat
And my hamster when it's out, drives my mum mad
Because it eats her mat.
My fish are cool they need no looking after
Just a pinch of food
When I get out of school.

Jamie Crooks (9)
St John's Primary School, Hillsborough

MY SISTER

My sister is fun
Better than a bun
She is cool
She is not a fool
Sometimes we play
On a sunny day
She can be bad
And really, really mad
But I love her
And she loves me
We are as happy as can be
We love to play hide and seek
I always hide
And she always seeks
But between it all we love each other
And I also have a little brother!

Rachel Morrow (9)
St John's Primary School, Hillsborough

MY FAMILY

My daddy works hard all week, only off on Sunday,
My mummy stays at home and works around the house,
Hannah is my sister she is so like a boy
She runs, she jumps and does not stop only when asleep
My brothers are Stuart, the oldest and Adam is the youngest,
My name is Chelsea, I am the eldest,
I love them all so very much
They love me too and we'll always be there for each other.

Chelsea Walker (9)
St John's Primary School, Hillsborough

MY BROTHER JAMES

My brother is mean
He shouldn't be seen,
He would drive you round the bed
And isn't a good friend.
He is very noisy
And extremely nosy,
He looks like a bat
But worse than a rat.
He is Mr Crossy
And very bossy,
He thinks he owns the place
And if he does
He needs a spot on his face.

Judith Caldwell (11)
St John's Primary School, Hillsborough

SISTERS AND GIRLS

Sisters, sisters everywhere
They get in your face, they get in your hair
They laugh and they giggle and walk with a wiggle
The old sisters put paint on their faces to make the boys chase them
The young ones cry all day, what can I say
There are girls who are tomboys and girls that are not
There are some sisters that are annoying and some that are fun
There are girls who are sporty and girls that are posh
I've got one sister but if I had two I would go *mad!*

Michael Allen (9)
St John's Primary School, Hillsborough

HORSES

Horse, horse, running fast,
Neigh, neigh to the field, eat grass
And run away
Disappearing like a little dot.
Go to the stable now, get ready for the race,
Get ready to go, go, go
Yes, you're winning yeah, yeah, yeah.
You have won the cup
You're put back to the field to have some fun
Then it's time for tea,
Then it's time for bed,
Neigh, neigh, neigh means goodnight
So neigh, neigh,

Hannah Walker (8)
St John's Primary School, Hillsborough

I'M IN A HURRY

Sorry no time for talking
I'm running, not walking.
Everyone get out of the way
I have to get home
Sometime today.
They tried to stop me
But I passed,
At last I'm home oh no!
I left my bag now I have
To go back again and
Get past all of them.

Steven McClune (8)
St John's Primary School, Hillsborough

WESTLIFE

Westlife are the best,
They're better than all the rest.
They even wear cool vests,
They would pass any test.

Westlife are so cool,
They would even make you drool.
The concert will be class,
It will be a blast.

Bryan is a dad
And it ain't half bad.
His wee girl is Molly
I bet she plays with dollies.

Especially for a flick
One became bald Nick
My favourite one is Shane
But I also like Kian . . .

The last one is Mark
Now he's a bright spark
He showed them all at school
That he was no fool.

Westlife is the band
The best in the land
And just for a start
Make me the Queen of your heart.

Rhianne Dillon (9)
St John's Primary School, Hillsborough

My Family

My name is Rachael
And I am eight.
I have two sisters
I think they are great.

I live with my parents
In a house down the road
And I never want
To live with a toad.

I go to church on Sundays
I don't much like Mondays.
I also go to Girl's Brigade
And love to drink lemonade.

My cousin is called Sarah
She's learning to walk.
It won't be long
Before she can talk.

My aunts and uncles
All love me lots
They buy me presents
Especially Jelly Tots.

My nana and papa
Who live up the lane.
Have a dog called Poppy
Who drives me insane.

My nanny and granda
Are not far away
I see them a lot
They like to play.

Rachael Robinson (8)
St John's Primary School, Hillsborough

ONE STORMY NIGHT

One stormy night as I stepped out . . .
The wind sliced open my cheeks like someone cutting through an apple
The rain came down like darts going through a board
The wind was screaming and roaring in my ear
The sky was like black chalk resting on the roofs
The thunder was deafening
It made the clouds come together and hailstone.
The wind was strong and angry,
No leaves were on the trees
Their branches were like witches fingers reaching out to the moon
The horrid tempest didn't stop till next day noon.

Sheena McLoughlin (11)
St Joseph's Convent Primary School, Newry

THE RATTLING RAILWAY

Faster than seagulls, faster than swans,
Rivers and mountains, shops and ponds,
Dashing like a dart over the hills,
Beautiful birds with beautiful bills.
Mighty mushrooms moulding by,
Delightful ducks swim and fly.

Slower than swans, slower than snails,
Rain and snow, wind and gales,
Dawdling along like a very old man,
The train is moving slow and calm,
Beautiful butterflies flutter around,
Now my feet can touch the ground.

Tara Wells (11)
St Joseph's Convent Primary School, Newry

ONE STORMY NIGHT

One very stormy night
As I crawled outside on that icy ground
I felt my heart being shot
By the coldness of this night.

It blew and blew
And the whistles of the wind
Began to make my ears go numb.
I could barely hear the roaring of the storm
As it roughly grabbed the trees
And swung them from side to side.

I felt as if I was in a big labyrinth,
The winds looked like fog.
Every time I took a step
Into that windy world
I felt as if I was falling through earth.

Suddenly there were no leaves
Left on the trees
As I walked away.

Níav-Cará Meegan (10)
St Joseph's Convent Primary School, Newry

EMOTIONS

Love is a gold, silk blanket smothering the world.
It smells like a garden of roses in summer.
Love tastes like a double chocolate cake with candy.
Love sounds like birds singing in the trees.
It feels like you are floating in the air in red, heart bubbles.

Hatred is red-hot, burning fire.
It tastes like big, swelling blisters in your throat.
Hatred smells like burnt sausages
It sounds like a roar of thunder.
Hatred feels like daggers through your heart.
Hatred lives in the heart of the Devil.

Kirsty Lowry (11)
St Joseph's Convent Primary School, Newry

ONE STORMY NIGHT

One threatening night as I nervously stumbled out
The devastating winds were screaming,
The terrifying skies were haunting the creatures of the night,
And making them toss and turn.
The lightning was blinding the moon
And the thunder deafening the sea
As its waves ran for safety.
The clouds gathered
And full of fright
They started to cry
And the wind smiled at their plight
As if it knew the night was so cold
Their tears would turn to ice.
Not a creature was in sight
Not a bird was in flight
On this horrible, menacing night.

Niamh Fearon (10)
St Joseph's Convent Primary School, Newry

THE HIRING FAIR

The children and adults huddle
The children desperately need a cuddle
The terror and the hate on their faces
As the farmer takes a few more paces
In the town
Faces do nothing but frown
In the cold and icy breeze
I'm sure all the children freeze
With expectations of the worst
Is this really a curse?

Roisin McCrink (10)
St Joseph's Convent Primary School, Newry

FROM A RAILWAY CARRIAGE

Zooming past the windowpane, driving in the winter rain,
Cars and buses fly quickly by, I'd miss them if I blinked an eye.
On I go towards the mountains covered now with thick, white snow;
Fields of green and rivers flowing, I wonder where those rivers go!
People move about the carriage to and fro, I watch them go,
Some are young and some are old with children being very bold.
With no stop, we pass a station on towards my destination,
Where that is I do not know, when I find out,
I'll tell you so!

Rebecca Watson (10)
St Joseph's Convent Primary School, Newry

WAITING

On a cold, blustery day
Standing terrified on the pebble road
Hundreds waiting, just waiting.

I am among these people
Terrified
Feet numb, standing here
Hundreds waiting, just waiting.

Waiting to be hired
Ears red with cold
Farmers nip and pinch
Hundreds waiting, just waiting
Just waiting.

Natasha Coyle (10)
St Joseph's Convent Primary School, Newry

SNOWDROPS

In the harsh winter winds
A little snowdrop appears
All by itself
Bobs its sleek and slender body to and fro.
Its dainty, snowy head dances
In the dark, cold world
Fragile body is tilted
Its bell head rings
In the face of cutting winds.

Elaine Hart (11)
St Joseph's Convent Primary School, Newry

MY DAD

My dad is a great man
He works hard all day
He will help anybody in any way
My dad doesn't like it when my brothers fight
So he puts them to bed and turns out the light
He takes us to youth club and football as well.
That's why I think my dad is *swell*.

Owen Curran (8)
St Joseph's Primary School, Strangford

THE MONSTER

I opened the door and there I saw
A horrible, ghastly sight.
A green, hairy monster, ten foot high
And then I started to cry.
My mum came running and fainted with shock
I slammed the door and bolted the lock
And never spoke of the monster again.

Harriet Conner (9)
St Joseph's Primary School, Strangford

THE MISTAKEN TEDDY

There's a monster in my cupboard
I know it's really there.
I told my mum when she was chewing gum
And I think she choked with scare!

I bet it's green and hairy
With sharp claws everywhere.
But when I took a look
It was my teddy bear.

Orla Kearney (9)
St Joseph's Primary School, Strangford

There's Something Under My Bed

There's something under my bed
And I don't know what it is
I hear these things at night
And it really gives me the shivers.
But I'm going to be brave tonight
And look under my bed . . .
And after all it was just my cat
I can't believe I was that scared!

Tara Laverty (9)
St Joseph's Primary School, Strangford

Winter

The wintertime is cold and dark
So we say goodbye to the lark
But we're not allowed out at night
The owl must be kept warm and fed
And be sure they have a warm bed.

Danny Savage (8)
St Joseph's Primary School, Strangford

My Mum Loves Flowers

Flowers, flowers everywhere
My mum loves flowers
Even if they are cheap or dear
My mum buys flowers
Dried flowers, big flowers, small flowers,
All year round.

Christina McConvey (8)
St Joseph's Primary School, Strangford

My Goldfish

My goldfish there are two
In their tank Buddy and Lou
Swimming around, water cool and clear
While eating breakfast we are so near.
Must go now, don't want to be late for school
Bye my friends in your water pool.

Conor Fitzsimons (9)
St Joseph's Primary School, Strangford

My Granda

I went to see my granda yesterday,
I think I'll go again today!
He is very old, maybe 60 or so,
He's not very big, maybe he'll grow!
He's got no teeth, his hair is grey,
But he's my granda and I love him anyway!

Niall McLaughlin (9)
St Joseph's Primary School, Strangford

SCHOOL HOLIDAYS

One thing I like best
Better than all the rest
Can you guess?
Yes! School holidays
Getting up whenever I like
Going for a spin on my bike.
Dressing any old way
After all it's my day
Lying all day under a hot sun
Eating a yummy, big jam bun.
Running with the other girls
Down at the funfair having a whirl
School holidays that's when to be
Time for me just to be free.

Anna Fitzsimons (8)
St Joseph's Primary School, Strangford

MY GRAMPA KERR

My grampa's really class
But can't run all that fast
He lives beside a beach
I would love to see him teach
Although he's very cross
So beware, he's the boss
My grampa spoils me rotten
So he's never to be forgotten.

Grainne Cassidy (9)
St Joseph's Primary School, Strangford

WEATHER FORECAST

Snow
Snow is falling from the sky
And landing softly on the ground.
It's coming from the clouds up high,
Listen carefully but you won't hear a sound.

Wind
Wind blows high and wind blows low.
You will not see it but sometimes hear it.
Where it comes from I don't know.
But I only like it when it blows a little bit.

Rain
Rain, rain go away I want to go out to play.
Rain can fall heavy, rain can fall light.
But I don't care how it falls, I can still have fun today.
As long as it doesn't hide all the sunlight.

Sunshine
Sun shines strong and sun shines bright,
It keeps us warm during the day.
When the sun fades it gets dark and is night,
But I can't wait for the sun to rise so that I can go out and play.

Nicole Killen (9)
St Joseph's Primary School, Downpatrick

MY GRAN

My gran is as funny as a monkey
Her hair is like a big world globe
Her eyes are like small music notes
Her face is like smooth sandpaper
When she walks she is like she is in a sack race

When she sits she is like a cushion
When she laughs she is like a man
When she sleeps she is like a baby
The best thing about my gran is she makes me laugh and sleep
And I love my gran.

Dean Killen (11)
St Joseph's Primary School, Downpatrick

THE HAUNTED HILL

On a haunted hill sits a haunted house,
We walked through the door, agh, it's a mouse!
The door creaked open, we heard a howl,
But it was only a great, grey, haunting owl.
As we walked through the room,
We saw a light, but it was only the moon.
Then we heard a great, big shriek,
We ran to the door
Boo! It was only great, big uncle Egore.

Hannah Lucas (10)
St Joseph's Primary School, Downpatrick

MY GRAN

My gran is as sweet as sugar.
Her hair is like a hawthorn tree.
Her eyes are like the deep blue
Her hair is like a bittersweet lemon
When she walks she is like a sweet woman
When she is sitting she is like a cat sleeping
When she laughs, she is like a teenager laughing.
When she sleeps she is like a cat purring
The best thing about my gran is she is very loving and kind.

Victoria Lucas (10)
St Joseph's Primary School, Downpatrick

MY GRAN

My gran is as bossy as an old, grumpy teacher is.
Her hair is like a curly, big, round bush.
Her eyes are like a cat's green eyes.
Her face is like a big, round cloud because she always cries.
When she walks her bum sticks out.
When she sits she makes a big hole in the chair.
When she laughs she is like a clown but her false teeth fall out
When she sleeps she always snores and whistles
The best thing about my gran is she always cuddles up with me.

Andrea Russell (10)
St Joseph's Primary School, Downpatrick

MY GRAN

My gran is as sweet as sugar.
Her hair is like a big bush with snow all over it.
Her eyes are like two bright stars.
Her face is like a crunched-up paper bag.
When she walks she is like a thin pencil walking.
When she sits she is like a tired sheep.
When she laughs she is like a laughing hyena.
When she sleeps she is like an angel sleeping.
The best thing about my gran is she never runs out of nice things to say.

Sean O'Rourke (10)
St Joseph's Primary School, Downpatrick

SUMMER

Summer is my name, running is my game
Running through the fields all day
Looking for some games to play.

The meadow flowers, they slowly sway
The farmers they collect their hay.

The children are outside at play
The mums are renewing last year's tan.

The lambs frolic in the fields
Rabbits hopping all around.

Naomi Killen (11)
St Joseph's Primary School, Downpatrick

THE SUN

I love the sun for when it shines
We have such fun with memorable times
We go to the beach and swim in the water
Mum puts her toe in and says, 'It's too cold.'
And I always say, 'Mum, you're too old!'
So that was my poem about the sun
I hope you enjoyed it and had lots of fun!

Tamara Lagatule (10)
St Joseph's Primary School, Downpatrick

SPRINGTIME

Lengthy showers of heavy rain,
Splashing off the windowpane.
Little children play out all day,
Because it is the month of May.
Baby lambs hopping in the fields,
As the farmer does his daily deals.
Daffodils and primroses in full bloom,
Maybe summer will be here soon.
But when I hear the little birds sing,
I know for sure that it is spring.

Joanne Reynolds (11)
St Joseph's Primary School, Downpatrick

MY WISH

I wish I was one of Santa's reindeer.
I wish I was a famous person like David Beckham.
I wish there was no fighting in the world.
I wish I could go on holiday.
I wish I could be Harry Potter.

Dane Fegan (8)
St Mary's Primary School, Killyleagh

MY WISH

I wish I went to see Britney Spears and also to be a footballer
I wish and wish to be a footballer
And play for Liverpool, Leeds, Chelsea and Rangers.

Rebecca Morrison (7)
St Mary's Primary School, Killyleagh

HAPPINESS

Happiness is when I go to school.
Happiness is when my family and I go on an outing.
I was happy when Man Utd beat Derby 5-0.

Ben Colgan (7)
St Mary's Primary School, Killyleagh

MY WISH

I wish I could play for Celtic and score lots of hat-tricks.
I wish I was a millionaire and I wish I could drive a car.

Conor Brennan (7)
St Mary's Primary School, Killyleagh

MY BAD BROTHER

M y bad brother always fights with me
Y ou might think he is bad - well he is.

B ut sometimes he is not so bad
A nd when I walk past his room he always says,
   'Do you want a fight?'
D isaster is what *he* is!

B rothers are so bad, I hate them!
R ather OK when my mum's about,
O pens my bedroom door when I'm doing my homework
   and starts to fight.
T here is one way I can get rid of him, by going out to play.
H e doesn't care if my mum yaps at him! He just carries on fighting,
E nters her bedroom and starts a fight with my sister,
R ages when I win a fight on his PlayStation!

Stacy Morrison (8)
St Mary's Primary School, Killyleagh

TWIN FRIENDS

G ary and Lee are twins - Gary's older,
A nd they're friends - sometimes!
R ather - I like them as brothers,
Y ou would too - I'm not lying!

A nd Gary and Lee are my best friends,
N ever in my life have I had better friends,
D id you know they were eight and *very bold?*

L ee is my second best friend,
E ven though we fight, we still get along.
E ven for the rest of my life we will still be friends!

Jamie Quinn (9)
St Mary's Primary School, Killyleagh

157

MY FAVOURITE FRIEND

My favourite friend
is called Mitsy.
She is part white
and the rest brown.
She lives with my
granny and grandad.
She stays in the yard
all the time.
When she's let out
for a run around the green
she always goes barking
mad after bottles,
but when she sees my mum and I
she comes rushing over to us
and jumps up on us.
She's nice and kind,
loves beautiful flowers
and butterflies
but she loves *me*.
That's my dog, Mitsy.

Tayler McMahon (9)
St Mary's Primary School, Killyleagh

HAPPINESS

Happiness is when it is my birthday.
Happiness is when my mum gets a new car.
Happiness is when I get new toys.
Happiness is when I go on holiday.

Happiness is meeting Robbie Williams.
Happiness is meeting the Liverpool team.
Happiness is playing with my friends.
Happiness is watching the sun go down.

Jamie Young (8)
St Mary's Primary School, Killyleagh

ABOUT A COMPUTER

A computer is . . .
Always confusing,
But now I've got
To know it,
It is very amusing.

Buttons are called keys
But it doesn't
Seem to like me
A screen to see through
But when I turn it on
It shuts out like
A beam.

When I print
It gives me a
Mouse to work it,
But not a house.

I like a
Computer very much.
Sometimes it
Doesn't like
Me to touch it.

Ryan Fegan (9)
St Mary's Primary School, Killyleagh

HAPPINESS POEM

Happiness is growing up
Happiness is running with your friends
Happiness is Christmas presents
Happiness is a new car to drive
Happiness is a new baby sister
Happiness is my dog.

Rebecca Kirk (7)
St Mary's Primary School, Killyleagh

MY WISH

I wish I was Harry Potter.
I wish I was David Beckham.
I wished I played for Man Utd.
I wish me and Jamie Y and Dylan were brothers.
I wish I was a millionaire.

Jamie Daly (8)
St Mary's Primary School, Killyleagh

I WISH

I wish I played for Belfast Giants,
I wish I were Harry Potter,
I wish I could drive a Subaru Impreza,
I wish I were rich,
I wish I were a king.

Dylan Vaughan (8)
St Mary's Primary School, Killyleagh

MY SISTER

My sister always tells me what to do
I'm like a little slave to her and her mirror.
'Stacy, brush my hair,' I'm like Cinderella.
'Do
    this,'
        'Do
            that,'
But last night I had a dream
That my sister and I had swapped around.
I was in her place,
It was only a dream but
It was good, I was saying,
'Do
    this,'
        'Do
            that,'
But then I woke up, then I realised something,
I'm glad I have her and she
        is my sister.

Stacy Gribben (9)
St Mary's Primary School, Killyleagh

HAPPINESS

Happiness is playing for Everton.
Happiness is having no school.
Happiness is going to Bangor.
Happiness is going with Dad to work.
Happiness is playing.
Happiness is drawing pictures.

Matthew Donnelly (8)
St Mary's Primary School, Killyleagh

I WISH I WAS A PIRATE

I wish I was
a pirate sailing
the seven seas.
I could find
hidden treasure and
fight more pirates.
I would beat them
and steal all their gold.
I wish I was a pirate
so I could be a captain
and could order
my shipmates about and
tell them to swab the deck.
That's why I want to be a pirate,
so cheerio me maties.

Steven Ward (10)
St Mary's Primary School, Killyleagh

MY WISH

I wish I was Harry Potter.
I wish I was a millionaire.
I wish I went to visit Britney Spears with Rebecca Morrison.
I wish I played for Rangers, Leeds and Chelsea.
I wish I had a horse to ride.
I wish I had a car or a motorbike.
I wish I had the video of Harry Potter.

Chelsea Reid (8)
St Mary's Primary School, Killyleagh

WITCH

Flying around her cauldron;
Stirring and casting
All sorts of spells.
Like . . .
Turning you into all sorts of things,
Like . . .
Maybe you don't want to be.
I don't know - and you don't know.
She's spiky, multicoloured
Dimples like all witches.
Knobbly knees
And has huge knobbly feet.
She doesn't have a black cloak though.
Has an orange coloured cloak streaming
Behind her in the breeze.

Shannon Newman Hunt (8)
St Mary's Primary School, Killyleagh

CELTIC

C   eltic are the *best* and always will be,
E   ven could beat Man City of course,
L   aarson is *brill* - always scores goals,
T   akes kicks and tales the ball round other players,
I   know Celtic are brill - 'cause they are best!
C   eltic are top of the Scottish League! Oh yes!

F   inally I am going to see them. They'll win!
C   an you ever, ever see them lose!

Stephanie Geddis (8)
St Mary's Primary School, Killyleagh

MY TEAM

M y favourite team
A t the top of the world,
N early the best in the state,
C hampions of the cup!
H e is the best, Van Nistelrooy,
E verybody in my family loves them.
'S uckers,' I shout to the other team.
T hey're tops! Are the best!
E very time they play I cheer,
R evenge is sweet, but winning is better.

U nited are the best
N ever do
I t will never stop, they will win every match.
T he cup will be theirs soon . . .
E verybody cheers for them, 'Go on you *Reds*
D o your best and you will win the *cup!'*

Adam Colgan (9)
St Mary's Primary School, Killyleagh

MY WISH

Happiness is when I get a new bike.
Happiness is getting a basketball set.
Happiness is going to Paris and seeing the Eiffel Tower.
Happiness is having a party.
Happiness is making friends.
Happiness is getting a new pet.
Happiness is being with my family.

Nicole Garrett (8)
St Mary's Primary School, Killyleagh

UNITED

M anaged by Ferguson
A t the top of the league,
N eville stops the goals,
C ame back from ten points behind the leaders.
H e's the one - David Beckham!
E verybody cheers when he scores,
S choles has powerful shots.
T he fans like Scholes and Beckham,
E veryone likes them,
R evenge - Man U always get back!

U nited always play a good match,
N o one boos United anymore,
I love *United!*
T he fans cheer Giggs and Van Nistelrooy
E very game - they come back and win,
D avid Beckham is England captain.

Jonathan Campbell (8)
St Mary's Primary School, Killyleagh

HAPPINESS

Happiness is when you get a present.
Happiness is when you get a one pound coin.
Happiness is when you get a cake.
Happiness is when you go to a birthday party.
Happiness is when you get jelly.
Happiness is when your friend plays with you.

Catherine McIlwrath (8)
St Mary's Primary School, Killyleagh

MY PET FISH

My pet fish is very greedy, so
I named him Feedy.
Once he gets fat
He might burst and blow away.
That would mean
I would have to get a new one.
Oh dear, oh dear!
He makes a noise like . . .
    P . . . P . . !
        P . . . P . . . !
            P . . . P . . . !
And that is my pet fish!

Melissa McComb (8)
St Mary's Primary School, Killyleagh

MICHAEL OWEN

M ichael is *the* best,
I cheer for him,
C an do everything,
H elped win the FA Cup,
A gainst Roma in the UEFA Cup as well!
E verything he does is good!
L eads the *Reds* to glory.

O ver one hundred Liverpool goals!
W onderful for England also,
E very goal he scores is great,
N ever misses many.

Ryan Williams (9)
St Mary's Primary School, Killyleagh

MY FAVOURITE TEAM

M anaged by Sir Alex,
A rsenal always beaten by Man U,
N early beat 'Boro,
C ertainly the best team in the world.
H ey, they are the best team ever,
E very match they play is great,
S o why don't you go and see the match,
T op of the league,
E veryone has to like them,
R ight everyone, they're back!

U nited scores two goals in five minutes,
N o more Man U losers,
I think they're *brill.*
T ry to beat them - if you can,
E very one of my friends supports Man U.
D o your best Man U and you will win the European Cup.

Caoimhe Gordon (9)
St Mary's Primary School, Killyleagh

SPORT

M an United are the best,
A t the top of the Premier League.
N o one can beat them.

U nited can beat everyone,
N early at the top of the league.
I like Man United,
T hey can beat Celtic.
E verybody in Man United is the best.
D id get beaten 2-0 at the weekend, though.

Kieran Sullivan (8)
St Mary's Primary School, Killyleagh

GOOSEBUMPS

One dark, dark night
The moon shone bright.
There was a house called Eeries Manor!
Nobody ever goes there!
It is ghostly!
Every night I hear screaming!
The monster's sharp teeth
Dig into the flesh
Of a helpless lady.
Found dead the next morning
In her bed.

Lee O'Prey (8)
St Mary's Primary School, Killyleagh

MY MUM

M y mum loves doing housework,
Y esterday she sent me to the shop for Daz.

M um likes her beauty sleep!
U gly nails she hates
M y mum's always on the go!

M um can't cook. She burns pasta!
Y ou might love my mum just like me
R eally she is the best
A nd that doesn't worry me.

Patrick Bennett (8)
St Mary's Primary School, Killyleagh

FOOTBALL CRAZY

F inishing the winner with no time left,
O ozing goals are the best,
O rdering manager shouting at you,
T raining is what to do,
B all at your feet, you miss a sitter,
A lemon drink before the match is very bitter,
L earn to play like men,
L eaving the bench, you say 'Amen.'

C razy goals finish the match,
R acing players are hard to catch,
A rguing with ref you get sent off,
Z ooming around in the cold, you cough
Y our manager will say, 'Hip, hip, hooray.'

Shane Walsh (9)
St Mary's Primary School, Killyleagh

CELTIC

C eltic are the greatest
O r rather the best!
M y whole family support them.
I got the new Celtic top,
N early have lost Laarson
G ot lovely style!

B ut they get beaten sometimes
A re fourth now in the league
C ome back in nearly every match
K ieran in my class supports them most!

Aisling Walsh (9)
St Mary's Primary School, Killyleagh

SIMBA

My pet dog called Simba,
Caught a frog,
Stood on a log,
And always jumps in bogs,
Oh what a *messy* dog!
Oh what should I do with him?
Should I give him away?
But the owner mightn't walk him every day!

My friend says yes,
But I say no.
Oh what should I do?
I love him too!

Melissa Kent (9)
St Mary's Primary School, Killyleagh

OLD TRAFFORD

M anaged by Sir Alex Ferguson,
A t the top of the league.
N early won the European Cup.

U nited are the best,
N early beat West Ham,
I 've always supported Man United,
T hey can beat Liverpool 5-0,
E arly in the morning I watch Man United play,
D avid Beckham is the best.

Gary O'Prey (8)
St Mary's Primary School, Killyleagh

THE SPECIAL STAR

The special star,
It shone so bright,
It guided me
Through all the night.

The star led me
To different places,
Where I saw lots
Of different faces.

There was a war
That very night,
The star didn't glow
Just as bright.

The next night,
The light went out,
The star had gone
To roam about.

Siobhan Kerley-Dunne (8)
St Oliver Plunkett Primary School, Newry

THE PAIN OF A BEE

Bees may sting,
Bees may hurt,
They give us honey but that's not enough,
They drive us insane,
Then give an awful pain.

Emer McGovern (8)
St Oliver Plunkett Primary School, Newry

THE RUNAWAY SHEEP

There was a dog that always barked,
Rex scared the sheep away
They ran so far and took so long
We couldn't find them for a day.

They travelled so far they landed on a mountain
Quickly they drank the water from a fountain.

The mother had lambs on her way,
They took so long to come that day,
They got to the field so late that night
Tired and wearily went to sleep under a light.

Michael Keenan (9)
St Oliver Plunkett Primary School, Newry

COLOUR OF A BUTTERFLY

Butterfly in the sky
Spread your wings up so high
You look so colourful,
You look so bright,
You shine like a rainbow during the night,
Be careful where you let your wings dry.

Amy McCann (8)
St Oliver Plunkett Primary School, Newry

MY HORSE BRANDY

Brandy is a gentle horse,
He is my best friend of course,
I like to take him for a trot,
But once he starts he just can't stop,

He eats his oats through the stable door,
He always comes to me for more,
Brandy is my special friend,
I hope our friendship never ends.

Eoin King (8)
St Oliver Plunkett Primary School, Newry

INSIDE MY HEAD

Try making an invention,
Far out of this world,
To get away with all my chores!

And there is my mum,
The workaholic,
Who shall be considered first.

There is an entirely new country,
With crystal white snow
And all peace lies within.

And there is a river,
Where fish grow large,
It flows so rapidly through the forest.

There is a free-style nature
And birds that sing all day,
The harmony rests all day.

There is no war, no abuse,
No intruder caught on tape
This is a happy world and shall rest
Forever more!

Matthew McDowell (10)
Tullymacarette Primary School

A KENNING

A travel killer
A fun thriller.

A face freezer
A children pleaser.

A bitter freezer
A glittered breezer.

An ice glazier
A robin bringer.

A lovely trickler
A wonder devisor.

Put these together
And I'm . . .

Snow.

Kelly Jordan (9)
Tullymacarette Primary School

IN A BOY'S HEAD

In it there is a marine trooper
Who looks a lot like me and
My big brother, Thomas.

And there's and adventurous pilot,
Flying a supersonic jet plane
That's me in the cockpit.

And there is a fabulous footballer
Who plays for the one and only Man United!
I am the new improved David Beckham!

Joshua McDowell (10)
Tullymacarette Primary School

TAG RUGBY

Out in the rain
    Playing the game
No writing, no reading!
    No *work* for me.

Get the ball
    And run for the line
If I can score
    The victory will be all *mine!*

I can't find a space
    I must not get stuck!
The players tackle me
    And end up in a ruck!

For me rugby's the *tops*
    Even better than Top Of The Pops!

Stephen Dickson (11)
Tullymacarette Primary School

I WENT TO HOLLAND

I went into the castle
And what did I see?
Skeletons and dungeons
Which frightened the life out of me.

I went in the dungeons
And what did I see?
A very scary ghost
Who said 'Boo' to me!

William Grafton (9)
Tullymacarette Primary School

I WENT TO SPAIN

I went to Spain
    And what did I see?
I saw human statues
    Staring at me!

Statues like Roman soldiers
    And even ET
Gold and bronze
    Gleaming at me.

Then at the zoo
    And what did I see?
Dolphins jumping high in the air
    Just to touch a ball on the roof.

Jill Poots (9)
Tullymacarette Primary School

A GIRL'S HEAD

There is a glistening shiny fabric
To make dazzling party clothes.

And a plan to do away with English
In this large class for me too.

A dark spooky shadow is above my head
Oops! I forgot it was a rainy day.

There is a land of peace where animals are free
And a flower that just will not grow for me.

A fight that has no end
And two nephews driving me round the bend!

Laura Clarke (10)
Tullymacarette Primary School

MY DOG YOGI!

My dog Yogi
Is really cool.
He loves to jump in the paddling pool.
He is five years old
He does what he's told.
He has a black coat
He likes getting soaked!

He is fast and small
But he's getting tall!
He likes his spuds and beans
But I don't like them at all!
He's the best dog I've ever had
The other dogs were always bad!

Neil Ward (11)
Tullymacarette Primary School

THE FUTURE IS NOW

The future is now and all war is gone
New York is fixed and so's the Pentagon.
The world is free from evil sins
Now the world's full of lovely things.
There are no taxes, nor money
To pay on this wonderful summer's day
Now this poem's over and half my mind is gone
Because these are my feelings now mankind's at its dawn.

Christopher Magill (10)
Tullymacarette Primary School

MY DOG HOLLY

My dog Holly,
Is such a wally!
She runs round the room,
Like a dog on a broom!

She is cute and cuddly
And is very bubbly.
She also really enjoys,
Playing with her toys.

Holly is the best!
She is better than the rest!
I gotta go now,
So I'll leave you with a bow-wow!

Antonia Baker (11)
Tullymacarette Primary School

MY DOG EDGAR

Edgar is my bestest buddy,
He's brown and white and really cuddly.
Edgar is a special friend,
Even though he drives my mum round the bend!
He eats us out,
That's one thing there's no doubt about!
He's really hyper,
He's three or four, just out of his diaper!
To me my Dalmatian is one in a million
Oh no! Make that a billion!
I could never have such a special friend,
Him and me will be friends to the end!

Pamela Kirk (10)
Tullymacarette Primary School

JOURNEYS

I think I'll go to Lapland today
    And dance on frozen lakes.
I think I'll also climb the ice
    And slide right down again.

I think I'll have a snowball fight
    With tons and tons of snow.
I think I'll touch the husky dogs
    Or even play with snow.

I think I'll go on a snow mobile
    Across a frozen lake
I think I'll go for a reindeer ride
    Slowly and gently we will glide.

I think I'll go see Santa Claus
    And maybe a few knickknacks
I think I'll go have my tea
    And then a Lapish story.

But now I've got to the end of my journey
    And fly back to my home
I really had a great adventure
    I'll look forward to another one!

Leanne Murphy (11)
Tullymacarette Primary School